D1598935

# Dawn of Memories

# Dawn of Memories

## The Meaning of Early Recollections in Life

Arthur J. Clark

ROWMAN & LITTLEFIELD PUBLISHERS, INC.
*Lanham • Boulder • New York • Toronto • Plymouth, UK*

Published by Rowman & Littlefield Publishers, Inc.
A wholly owned subsidary of The Rowman & Littlefield Publishing
Group, Inc.
4501 Forbes Boulevard, Suite 200, Lanham, Maryland 20706
www.rowman.com

10 Thornbury Road, Plymouth PL6 7PP, United Kingdom

British Library Cataloguing in Publication Information Available

**Library of Congress Cataloging-in-Publication Data**

Clark, Arthur J.
  Dawn of memories : the meaning of early recollections in life / Arthur J.
Clark.
     pages cm
  Includes bibliographical references and index.
  ISBN 978-1-4422-2180-2 (cloth : alk. paper) — ISBN
978-1-4422-2181-9 (ebook)  1.  Reminiscing.  2.  Recollection
(Psychology) 3.  Children—Biography. 4.  Counseling.  I. Title.
  BF378.R44C55 2013
  153.1'2—dc23

                                                                    2013002029

∞™ The paper used in this publication meets the minimum requirements
of American National Standard for Information Sciences—Permanence of
Paper for Printed Library Materials, ANSI/NISO Z39.48-1992.

Printed in the United States of America

To my wife, Marybeth.

Although I am able to summon only a small number of recollections from my early childhood,

I readily recall abundant and beautiful memories with you over the forty years of our lives together.

# Contents

# Introduction

Toward the beginning of my career in counseling and psychology, I learned that it is possible to gain insights into human personality through the interpretation of the first memories of life. Without much experience in the assessment of early recollections, it occurred to me that my father would make an appropriate candidate with whom to try out my novice skill, so I asked him to recall one of his first remembrances. In reaction to my query he looked at me and stated in a somewhat serious tone: "I remember my father giving me a rabbit as a present. I held him in my arms, and I could see the rabbit's eyes and ears." I didn't find my father's memory surprising because, although we lived in a large city when growing up, he always kept rabbits in a hutch next to our family home. What I did not anticipate, however, was my father's response to my follow-up question related to his feelings when holding the rabbit. Rather than experiencing excitement, joy, or some other uplifting emotion, he said, "I felt responsible for taking care of the rabbit." Instantly I was struck by how that statement captured my father's way of being and outlook on life. Only as I grew into an adult did I fully appreciate his dutiful and loving commitment to my mother and our family of six children. I cannot recall him missing a day of work as a machinist or complaining about the often-harsh conditions of his factory job. To make ends meet, he also ran a bicycle repair shop out of the garage in the back of our house and spent hours in the evenings and on weekends fixing bikes.

Perhaps like most people, I was skeptical when I first heard that the appraisal of early recollections has the potential to reveal glimpses into an individual's deepest nature. After all, the first memories of life seem to be a random assortment of visualized events from a person's past and appear to lack any coherent sequence or meaning. Although I was familiar with some of the vast knowledge and information on the topic of human memory, learning about early recollections as a personality appraisal tool was new to me. In my therapeutic training, I had been introduced to the Rorschach, the famous ink blot test. Like the Rorschach, early recollections are a *projective technique*. Theoretically, projective techniques have a capacity for people to project aspects of their personality functioning into vague and ambiguous stimuli, such as ink blot images or verbal responses in the manner that my father did when asked about first memories.

Throughout the thirty-five years since asking my father to recount his first memory, I have interpreted thousands of early childhood memories with individuals and have seen how an awareness of the meaning of the remembrances enhances self-understanding and fosters human development and interpersonal relationships. In my counseling practice, I have regularly employed this projective technique with a diverse range of clients. With at-risk adolescents, couples with strains in their relationship, persons with substance abuse problems, and various other treatment concerns, I have found early recollections to be an invaluable resource for gaining insights into human personality. In my current position as a university professor, providing instruction on the projective technique to a generation of graduate students in school and mental health counseling has been gratifying for me. I have also written extensively on first childhood memories in the psychological literature and made numerous presentations on the topic to practitioners. Outside of a professional role, I have often had the pleasure of introducing early recollections at social gatherings and revaluating the remembrances of friends and relatives. Invariably these enlightening exchanges led to lively discussions on the nature and meaning of first memories.

In recent years, my goal has been to write a thought-provoking book for the general public on the first memories of childhood. My intent was to share the intriguing and enlightening nature of the remembrances beyond their use by practitioners with clients experiencing emotional distress. Having already written a book on the topic with a counseling and psychotherapy focus, I knew that I could draw from my considerable experience and scholarship on early recollections in composing a new volume. At the same time, I was also aware that there are important differences when writing for skilled practitioners in contrast to a public audience. Consequently, I have written *Dawn of Memories* in what I hope is an approachable and engaging style for individuals without a background in counseling and psychology. In this book, after a discussion of the intriguing historical literature on the first memories of childhood, I introduce a new model for interpreting early recollections that is clear and understandable for a broad readership. In *Dawn of Memories*, I sincerely hope that you enjoy your journey into the fascinating realm of exploring the meaning of early recollections in life.

*Part I*

# ORIGINS AND INVESTIGATIONS OF EARLY RECOLLECTIONS

*Chapter One*

# Unlocking the Front Door

## *An Introduction to Early Recollections*

How we remember, what we remember, and why we remember forms the most personal map of our individuality.

—Christina Baldwin[1]

"Think back to a long time ago when you were little, and try to re-call one of your earliest memories, one of the first things that you can remember."[2] For most people, this request immediately evokes the visual image of seeing oneself as a young child interacting with a person or an object from a perspective of about five to seven feet away. Curiously, these renderings of early recollections usually lack a striking or conspicuous quality that would make them particularly memorable for a person. Rather, they most often depict ordinary and everyday events. It is also surprising that, in spite of being surrounded by sounds and noises in the early childhood years, the vast majority of first memories brought to mind by a person occur in silence. Unlike remembrances from later periods in life that emerge as sequential and continuous in time, first memories are chronologically disconnected from one another and seem to be a random assortment. Although in-dividuals engage in thousands of experiences in life prior to the age of eight, it is unusual for a person to summon more than a handful of remembrances from this formative period.[3] Intriguingly, memories from the earliest years that emerge into consciousness seem to endure as the same recollections with a minimal degree of change over an

7

individual's life span.[4] Considering that first memories are rather ordinary in content, almost always without sound, disconnected, sparse,
and relatively stable, what may be the most puzzling thought is that
these particular recollections are even remembered at all.

Initial memories of life have long been a fascinating topic of
everyday speculation and psychological inquiry. Yet, until the beginning of the 1900s, when addressed in writings by Alfred Adler,
the profound and revealing quality of early recollections for the
assessment of personality had been largely undetected and unex-
plored. Adler, a Viennese physician and psychotherapist, developed
a revolutionary theory relating to why individuals recall memories
from early childhood, and why they are recollected in a distinctive
and unique way. Adler rejected the then contemporary notion that
first remembrances are merely a meaningless collection of conscious
memories with no discernible function or consequence. Instead, he
asserted that the meaning or the purpose of early recollections is to
enlighten individuals as to what life is about and to provide a tested
means for dealing with the challenges of living.[5] In his professional
and popular works, Adler chronicled how early remembrances have
a potential to yield insights into a person's deepest nature.

For more one hundred years, a vast collection of written commentaries and research on early childhood memories has been published around the world.[6] As a feature of this literature, a number
of historical figures have disclosed first remembrances which have
appeared in various accounts of their lives. In turn, researchers uti-
lized interpretations of the early recollections to provide glimpses
into the personalities of Albert Einstein, Benjamin Franklin, Martin
Luther King Jr., and other celebrated individuals.[7] As an addition
to the literature of historical figures, in an autobiographical render-
ing, Jimmy Carter, the thirty-ninth president of the United States,
recounts one of his first memories, illuminating key aspects of his
personality and his enduring outlook on life.

Although I was born in Plains and actually lived next door to my future wife, Roselynn, when she was a baby, the first thing I remember

clearly was when I was four years old and my father took us to show us our new home on the farm. There were four of us, including my sister, Gloria, who was two years younger than I. The front door was locked when we got there, and Daddy realized that he had forgotten the key. He tried to raise one of the windows that opened onto the front porch, but a wooden bar on the inside let it come up only about six inches. So he slid me through the crack and I came around to unlock the door from the inside. The approval of my father for my first useful act has always been one of my most vivid memories.[8]

When interpreting the meaning of this early recollection, assuming an empathic stance helps an individual grasp what it was like to be Jimmy Carter for a moment in time. Through an act of imagination, the possibility exists to envision Jimmy and his family excitedly arriving at the farmhouse and feeling emotionally let down when they are unable to enter the locked front door of their new home. We can picture Jimmy, with his father's assistance, shimmying through the narrow space in the open window. As Jimmy scampers across the house, his family members cheer him on. In what might be the most vivid part of the memory, we see Jimmy, smiling broadly, as he pulls open the front door. As each person quickly files into the house, they gratefully acknowledge Jimmy for his helpful accomplishment.

Allowing Jimmy's early recollection to resonate internally builds a readiness to assume a more analytical or detached posture to interpret the possible meaning of the remembrance. From a thematic perspective, Jimmy demonstrates optimism and initiative in overcoming an obstacle and resourcefully solving a problem that enables his family to get into their house. As the central figure in the first memory, Jimmy responsibly accomplishes his goal to the acclaim of his father and other family members. Giving consideration to perceptual details in the remembrance, the specific location in Plains, Georgia, stands out as a special place, and the farmhouse with its front porch is beckoning for all of the family members. Notable objects in the memory include the specific features of the house: the window, wooden bar, porch, and the front door. From a sensory perspective, the memory evokes a clear visual image, and Jimmy's sense of touch is also prominent as his father lifts him up to the window and Jimmy eagerly slides though. Additional details in the recollection include a reference to Roselynn, Gloria and her age, and the particular size of the window opening.

The final step in interpreting the meaning of Carter's first memory is to relate its core or central theme and the telling details to his personality and life experiences. The thematic focus of dutiful action and sense of accomplishment in Carter's early recollection reflects a pattern of behavior that was evident in his presidential and postpresidential years. In his single term as president of the United States, Carter was tireless and tenacious in his attempts to overcome obstacles and solve problems. Nuclear arms control, human rights, global health, energy conservation, government efficiency, and industry deregulation were among a number of issues tackled by Carter and his administration.[9] Yet, in spite of Carter's diligence and determination, sweeping forces and events outpaced his attentive resolve to find solutions to looming challenges. On a national level, double-digit unemployment and skyrocketing inflation became entrenched. As part of his personal response, Carter was publically scorned for suggesting that the lights and air conditioning be turned off in the White House to save costs and for becoming bogged down in details through a micromanagement style. Although his single effort paid off in his first memory, Carter's more solitary and pedantic actions often produced mixed results on a global scale. Carter was criticized for his foreign policy weakness and preoccupation with futile plans to free American hostages in Iran after the seizure of the U.S. Embassy. At the same time, the doggedness and self-reliance seen in his early recollection were mobilized when Carter almost singlehandedly brought about the Camp David accord in September 1978. Engaging an unflagging work ethic and knowledge of details, Carter spent ten days mediating an agreement between Israel and Egypt when it appeared that the diplomatic negotiations would break off early in the peace talks.[10]

After leaving the presidency, Carter persisted in attempting to solve problems and to help others through an action orientation as he did in his first remembrance. Through his appetite for work and desire to be useful, Carter devoted himself to advancing human causes around the world. With his wife, Roselynn, Carter founded the Carter Center to fight poverty, control diseases, and promote peace in developing nations. As a prominent figure with Habitat for Humanity, Carter spent hundreds of volunteer hours in construction projects using his hands in a way that was similar to his efforts in his first memory. During this period, Carter also wrote more than twenty books. All of his efforts culminated in October 2002, when he was awarded the Nobel Peace Prize in Oslo.[11] When Carter left the presidency, he went home to Plains, Georgia. Home, as depicted in his early recollection, has always been a special place for Carter with his deep affection for the land and its people. As in his first memory, Carter continued to make use of his hands and the sense of touch by crafting cedar chests, cabinets, and duck decoys.

Although Jimmy Carter's early recollection suggests aspects of his personality functioning and perceptual sensitivities, the narration lacks the vivid quality that typically resonates when an individual relates a memory on a face-to-face basis. Verbal and nonverbal communication, in such forms as gestures, vocal tone, and facial expressions, contribute to empathically understanding a person's remembrance. A physical presence and interpersonal exchange also allows for follow-up questions such as, "What part do you remember most in the memory?" Evaluating more than one recollection of an individual is also preferable, as this increases the scope of a way of knowing. Becoming familiar with the extensive literature on early memories is another vehicle for understanding implications and meanings of the remembrances.

Since the first investigation on early childhood memories conducted in the late 1800s, there has been a continuous outpouring of research and publications on the topic. Consideration has been given to such questions as, "What is the earliest age that a person can recall a memory?" and "Are pleasant early memories more common than unpleasant ones?" The study of human personality dimensions, which emerge through the assessment of early recollections, has been another prominent research focus. Personality qualities, such as the level of an individual's activity and initiative, optimism and pessimism, and conscientiousness, are important factors in interpreting first memories and in the quality of life. Clarifying the meaning of the five sense modalities, color, place or location, and physical objects made reference to in early recollections have also been found to provide insights into how a person perceives and experiences the world. In another direction, there have been numerous inquiries on first memories involving individuals with emotional or psychological disorders, and these findings have been applied to treatment practices and advances in counseling and psychotherapy.

In *Dawn of Memories: The Meaning of Early Recollections in Life*, I attempt to draw together the vast knowledge about early childhood and integrate the findings in a framework that provides an avenue for understanding personal capacities and potentialities. Part I, "Origin and Investigations of First Memories," includes an introduction, historical perspectives, and a view of Alfred Adler's original and innovative work relating to early recollections. Part II, "Interpretation and Meanings of Early Recollections," begins by recounting a first memory of Benjamin Franklin and then provides an overview of the *Dawn of Memories* model for understanding the meaning of early recollections in the context of Franklin's life. Further chapters detail how core themes, personality dimensions, and perceptual modalities relate to first memories and how an awareness of the factors have a potential to enhance an individual's well-being and mental health. Part III, "Traditions and Practices of Early Recollections," focuses on early childhood memories of eminent historical figures, the use of first remembrances in counseling and therapeutic contexts, and employing early recollections in one's life to promote self-understanding and personal development.

Early recollections reveal what is most meaningful to a person by exploring one's past through ingrained images. Recounting a first memory reveals a set of circumstances that are unique to an individual, composed as a young girl or a young boy. There is a personal story inherent in a remembrance, which contributes to defining the individuality of the person. In turning next to the century-long research on first memories, a journey begins that continues today into the captivating realm of the dawn of memories.

# Chapter Two

# Looking Forward by Thinking Back

## *Historical Perspectives on First Memories*

> My first memories are fragmented and isolated and contemporaneous, as though one remembered some first moments of the Seven Days. It seems as if time had not yet been created, for all thoughts connected with emotion and place without sequence.
>
> —William Butler Yeats[1]

During the winter, Caroline Miles, a psychology instructor at Wellesley College, asked a random group of students and faculty at the college in Massachusetts, "What is the earliest thing you are sure you can remember?"[2] Of the nearly one hundred persons providing written reactions to this question, almost one-half recalled a birth or death in the family, being frightened or hurt, or memories of an illness. Individuals also remembered various activities like playing in a garden, dressing up a dog, or trying to make a chicken swim. Many other responses did not fall into any particular category and involved such objects as a horse and a carriage, a sword, and a kitten. In her study, Miles also evaluated aspects of individual development beyond first remembrances by asking questions such as "What were your favorite games when a child?" and "What is your favorite color?"

Of the hundreds of investigations focusing on early childhood memories published after Miles's work, she was the first to give formal consideration to the topic. In addition to making reference to various themes and objects in their first remembrances, individuals recalled sensory impressions and estimated their chronological ages at the time of the experiences in early childhood. Vision was the most frequent sense expression identified in the first remembrances. Miles thought that sensations of sight were the prominent sense modality because a person's focus of attention typically turns to what's seen in most circumstances. Yet, even though they emerged in far fewer instances in comparison to visual images, other sensory expressions were also evoked in the first memories in combination with sight modalities. In an illustration involving multiple senses, an individual recalls being ill in an early childhood memory. The child is in a dark room with a single candle in the night and he sees his mother's face as she attentively bends over. The father's voice is heard as he is carrying the medicine, and the sick child remembers the taste of the medicine.[3]

Miles found that in early memories the senses dominate to the extent that they seem to diminish the capacity of the individuals to focus on their emotions in their remembrances. Yet, even with this explanation, she was still curious about difficulties people had in remembering emotional reactions relating to their recollections. Of the small number who made reference to an emotion in their first memories, one person remembered feeling angry when a necklace was stolen, and two others recalled feelings of pleasure upon receiving a present. With respect to chronological age in first memories, individuals were asked "How old were you?" The average age for the respondents in their remembrances was found to be just over three years.

In 1895, Victor Henri, a French psychologist, sent out a call to readers of two psychological journals to respond to a series of eleven questions relating to the topic of first memories.[4] Henri was joined with his wife, Catherine, in publishing the results of the inquiries, and they were the first researchers to devote an exclusive focus to recollections in early childhood. Originally appearing in the periodical *L'Année Psychologique*, the study was translated into

English in 1898 for the *Popular Science Monthly*.[5] The Henris gave consideration to such questions as the clarity, age, and significance of first memories. Ranging in age from sixteen to sixty-five years, more than one hundred people from Europe and the United States provided replies to the Henris' inquiries. Among the questions in the survey were, "What is the earliest recollection of your childhood? Please describe it as fully as possible. How clear is it, and what was your age when the fact recollected occurred?"[6] Interestingly, of the first memories disclosed, most respondents recalled brief visual scenes lasting only an instant or a few minutes duration. Recollections comprising lengthier periods of time were rare, and when reported they included fragmented time gaps in the narration of the remembrance rather than a continuous story.

Another unexpected finding by the Henris related to the significant time that existed between an individual's report of a first and second early memory. For most persons, the time interval between the remembrances was found to be more than a year, and in some instances it extended up to five years. In a few cases the respondents reported a month or two difference in time between their recollections but were uncertain as to the order of the first or second memory.[7] Thus, the Henris found that early childhood memories tend to be scattered chronologically and lacked a serial or sequential order that is commonly present in memories from later periods of life.

Following a line of inquiry similar to Miles's survey, Henri and Henri gave particular attention to sensory functioning in first memories. Among Henris' initial eleven questions to each respondent, two pertained to visual and auditory impressions. In employing a cue or a prompt, individuals were asked about particular sense modalities which might emerge in their early memories:

> Do you have good *visual* representations of objects in general; viz., can you form a visual image of an apple or a lamp, etc.?
>
> Do you have good *auditory* representations (of sounds), viz., have you auditory representations of the voices of your friends?[8]

In results close to those reported by Miles, the Henris found that most respondents had strong visual and weaker auditory remembrances. By specifically eliciting visual or auditory memories, however, this type of direct questioning has a potential to trigger a sensory impression which may or may not be brought to mind when asking a person to spontaneously recall an early recollection without cuing or prompting.

In an example of an early memory with a visual emphasis, a person depicted the following scene: "A large room, with a fire on the hearth, and the ceiling and walls in the dark; an aged lady sitting before the fire, which shines brightly upon her. I am sitting in her lap. On the floor is a toy, a sheep with gilded horns. I have on red stockings, and have hold of the woman's nose. It is a large, flabby nose; the woman's face is wrinkled, her hair is white, and she wears spectacles."[9] The colors present in the recollection intensify its visual imagery, and the objects are visually distinctive. As another sensory modality, the individual's sense of touch is also notable in the remembrance.

Although Henri and Henri did not ask the respondents to identify feelings in their first memories, they did find that persons expressed a range of emotions in their remembrances, such as fear, terror, shame, joy, and curiosity.[10] With some individuals, however, they may have been aware of having a particular emotion, but they did not experience the feeling and could only describe it in general terms. In other instances, persons actively felt the same emotion they had as a young child in their early memories. One respondent wrote, for example, "My first recollection was the astonishment I felt one morning at seeing the roofs without snow upon them. I thought they must be white all the year round, and I conceive now very clearly my surprise when I found that they were not. I was then three or four years old."[11]

After the groundwork was established on early childhood memories in the late 1800s, numerous investigators subsequently focused on topics that Miles and the Henris introduced in their initial explorations of the remembrances. In particular, a person's age, emotional reactions, and sensory impressions in first remembrances became subjects of inquiry of a wide range of publications throughout the twentieth and into the twenty-first century. Although not a direct focus in the earliest investigations, the pleasantness or unpleasantness of early memories and various other topics have been a prominent area of interest among subsequent researchers.

## AGE AND FIRST MEMORIES

How far back in age and time is it possible for an individual to remember? Trying to bring to mind one's own initial memory from early childhood is a pursuit that many people have entertained at some point in their lives. The answer to this question has also been an enduring line of inquiry in the literature on early memories for more than a century.[12] Verifying the time or date of the very first memory can be challenging because the recollection of an event is infrequently linked to a calendar year in the life of an individual. When researchers attempt to establish a person's age in a memory, taking note of specific circumstances in the recollection is possibly revealing. For example, moving to a new house, the birth of a younger sibling, or a death in the family may indicate a known date of an early memory. As another means of verification, individuals, such as a parent or another adult, may verbally confirm the chronological occurrence of an individual's early recollection. An alternative method of determination simply involves asking someone to estimate her age in a first remembrance.

Numerous researchers agree that most people recall their very earliest memory between three and four years of age.[13] At the same time, the age range of the first recollection of life is broad and extends through the seventh year. Various surveys indicate that approximately 1 percent of individuals are able to bring to mind memories before their third birthday. Another consistent finding is that the average age for identifying their earliest remembrance appears to be slightly lower for females than for males.[14] In a representative study conducted in the early 1940s, the average age for first recall was between the third and fourth years of life.[15]

## EMOTIONS AND FIRST MEMORIES

Most renderings of early childhood memories involve an expression of feelings. This is not surprising because the retention and recall of remembrances often relates to their emotional impact on individuals at a point in time. In other words, people are more likely to retain in their memory experiences or impressions that evoke affective reactions in an immediate context. Emotions also serve a primary function in stimulating and motivating human behavior across the life span. Consequently, feeling responses in first memories may prompt a person to pursue or avoid various actions in the remembrances. Individuals also react to events in their early recollections with a broad range of affective responses and emotional intensities. At the same time, certain emotions emerge with a relative degree of frequency in first memories.[16] Fear, joy, and anger are prominent in the remembrances, as are other emotional reactions including wonder and curiosity, sorrow and disappointment, and shame and guilt. Dozens of other affective states may be added to this array that differ in accordance with the unique character of a person's early recollection.

The emotion of fear is notable in early memories and involves variations of anxiety and worry. Numerous experiences can elicit these reactions in the remembrances, such as receiving punishment or feeling isolated or abandoned. In a fearful example, an individual recalls, "I remember sitting in the front seat of an old black car with my father. He kept turning the key, but the car wouldn't go. Then he started yelling and hitting the steering wheel with his fists. It was so scary." In a contrasting direction, the expression of the prominent emotion of joy in a first remembrance includes variations of delight and elation. Events such as being given a gift and receiving attention give rise to joyful affect. In an uplifting illustration, an individual recounts, "I was in my bedroom and the sun was just coming up. It had snowed outside, but it was nice and warm in my bed. I heard my parents downstairs, and I could smell the pancakes that my mother was making for breakfast." The expression of anger in early memories is another conspicuous emotion that includes variations of hate and resentment. A person's report of anger is usually the result of an interaction with others or a tangible object coupled with being thwarted, injured, or coerced. As an example, an individual relates, "It was snowing, and my older brother was getting on his coat to go out, but my mother wouldn't let me go with him. I was really mad at my mother, but she wouldn't change her mind."

## PLEASANT AND UNPLEASANT EARLY MEMORIES

When recounting early remembrances, do people more often remember agreeable or disagreeable memories? Sigmund Freud thought that people tend to repress unpleasant memories, and this view has a logical and intuitive appeal.[17] It seems to make sense that individuals would recall more positive recollections because they generally elicit pleasant moods that have an elevating effect. There is also an adaptive function that is sustaining when human beings recollect memories that convey hope and optimism in order to cope with life challenges and adversities. At the end of the nineteenth century, F. W. Colegrove, a Fellow at Clark University, was the first researcher to investigate the qualitative nature of early memories by asking the survey question, "Do you recall pleasant or unpleasant experiences better?"[18] Colegrove found that more often individuals tend to bring to mind pleasant first remembrances.

In a contrasting direction, however, some researchers did not agree that pleasant memories are more common than unpleasant remembrances in early memories. In 1928, Kate Gordon, a psychology professor at the University of California at Los Angeles, reported a preponderance of unpleasant first memories in her comprehensive study.[19] Gordon also made the critical point, "From the point of view of general theory, if human beings are in quest of the pleasant it would seem to be just as important to remember what to avoid as to remember what to pursue."[20] In this respect, an unpleasant memory potentially offers a cautionary measure to a person regarding what might be potentially threatening or harmful. In the service of the individual, this can ultimately be adaptive. As an example, in an early childhood recollection a middle-age man recalls being nipped in the hand when feeding a squirrel after being warned by his parents not to get too close to the animal. His memory involved a thematic focus of taking heed of trustworthy authority figures and learning from mistakes.

Another aspect of the unpleasant or pleasant recall of first memories controversy relates to the nature of the environment in early childhood experiences. Harsh or oppressive conditions in the first years of a person's life would generally seem likely to contribute to less pleasant early recollections. In this regard, when considering social and cultural forces, several researchers found that individuals had significantly more unpleasant early memories when raised in home and community environments involving poverty, violence, and neglect.[21] Consider the possible influences on one's outlook on life in the following early recollection of a young adult client in treatment for depression: "I'm in my crib, wet, soiled, and wet. My mother comes in the room and starts yelling at me." The feeling tone of first memories may also fall in a neutral category between pleasant and unpleasant experiences. For example, a person recalls, "I was looking out the window of my bedroom at the trees outside. Not much was happening." When considering the affective dimension of early recollections among individuals, a comprehensive survey published in 1948 seems to be representative in round numbers: 50 percent pleasant, 30 percent unpleasant, and 20 percent neutral.[22]

## SENSORY MODALITIES AND EARLY MEMORIES

When recounting an early recollection, a person almost invariably forms a visual image of oneself as a young child participating in some type of activity. Visualizing and narrating an event typically occurs from the perspective of an individual's current age—although the early childhood experience took place possibly decades earlier. After relating a first memory, the visual scene fades from consciousness, and the momentary occurrence of revisiting a setting which took place in the first years of life concludes. The visual channel is dominant in early memories, as the other senses emerge with far less frequency. What might be surprising in this regard is that recollections from the first years of life almost always occur in silence.[23] In spite of the countless bedtime stories, lullabies, and other auditory communications that children typically hear in their first years, sounds are relatively rare in first memories. In this respect, for most people, calling to mind an early recollection is similar to watching a brief episode of a silent movie.

In addition to the aural modality, other sense impressions are also far less common in first memories. In descending order of occurrence, the mention of touch, smell, and taste are found in single-digit numbers of early remembrances out of one hundred for each modality.[24] It is interesting to speculate why first memories generally lack a representation of a range of senses exclusive of vision. Certainly, children typically are exposed to innumerable sense experiences in their early years of development. For example, interactions of touch and being touched and instances of being fed and eating fall in the thousands for virtually all young children. One plausible line of reasoning for the scarcity of sense impressions other than vision is that a person retains remembrances from early childhood that are deemed essential or even crucial. Therefore, other senses, in comparison with sight, may be less critical to an individual to navigate or comport with life.

At the same time, early memories certainly involve senses beyond sight and pose the question of what weight should be given to them?

One possible explanation is that particular senses are intrinsic to an individual's functioning or unique outlook on life. As an example, Kyle Weaver, a mental health counselor, recalls an early recollection with a prominent auditory focus. "I was at an ice skating rink with my father; I was probably three or four years old. I was just learning to skate and had fallen down. Another man in the memory tried to cheer me up by pretending to 'water ski' on his skates. I distinctly remember him asking if I wanted to see him water ski. I remember the sound of his ice skates carving deep grooves in the ice, the crunching sound it made was awe-striking for me. That crunching sound was an instant obsession, and from then on, even today, when I get a chance to get out on the ice and skate, I deliberately take hard strides so I can hear and feel the ice crunching beneath my skate blades."

In response to the meaning of sound in his early recollection, Kyle states, "As many people know shortly after meeting me, I am very auditory. I learn best not by reading, but by listening. I enjoy talking to no end. In the right group of close friends, I am most definitely the jokester who never stops talking. No matter what my mood, I listen to music. I have a thirst for music in my gut. I also talk to myself in my head in the sense that I have conversations with myself." It is apparent for Kyle, and for others with prominent sense impressions in their early memories, that particular modalities can be influential as a distinctive value and an orienting focus in life.

## Chapter Three

# The Story of My Life

## *Personality Dynamics, Early Recollections, and Alfred Adler*

Scarcely any one understands a first memory; and most people are therefore able to confess their purpose in life, their relationship to others and their view of the environment in a perfectly neutral and unembarrassed manner through their first memories.

—Alfred Adler[1]

In Austria during the winter of 1911, Alfred Adler addressed a gathering of the Vienna Psychoanalytic Society on his innovative theoretical positions which had become controversial among the members of the professional group. In one of his lecture presentations, Adler made his initial comments on the relationship of first remembrances to understanding personality functioning and human development. As president of the society, Adler stated, "A person's true attitude toward life can be discerned from his earliest dreams and recollected experiences, proving that such memories are also constructed according to a planful procedure."[2] At the time, Adler generally used dreams in combination with early recollections in his therapeutic treatment approach for gaining insights into a patient's way of being. The winter meetings of the Viennese association were also notable because they marked Adler's acrimonious break with Sigmund Freud due to critical differences in their theoretical viewpoints and treatment approaches. In Freud's formulations, infantile sexuality was preeminent in understanding human behavior on a normal and pathological basis, whereas Adler felt that sexuality was less prominent in terms of a developmental influence.

Freud thought that early childhood memories frequently relate to and conceal troubling, sexually charged conflicts. Surface or manifest memories, according to Freud, often serve as an unconscious screen for more disturbing or traumatic experiences at a latent or deeper level. In this regard, Freud states, "The indifferent memories of childhood owe their existence to a process of displacement: they are substitutes, in [mnemic] reproduction, for other impressions which are really significant."[3] In contrast to Freud's position, which minimized the importance of the memories that more readily emerge into an individual's consciousness, Adler makes the point that, "There are no indifferent or nonsensical recollections."[4] In this respect, remembrances that a person immediately discloses has a therapeutic value in terms of empathic understanding and treatment implications. Early memories reveal clues or hints about his personality and pattern of life. Adler found that people are usually receptive when asked about their early recollections and are willing to openly discuss them. Individuals are almost always unaware of the hidden psychological meanings in their remembrances and simply acknowledge the memories as factual information.

By the summer of 1911, the incompatible views of Adler and Freud had culminated in a major rift and led to Adler's resignation from the Vienna Psychoanalytic Society.[5] Within a period of weeks, Adler and a small group of followers who also resigned with him began to organize a separate association with the name of the Society for Free Psychoanalytic Study. Adopting the new designation of "individual psychology" in 1912, Adler continued to expand and expound upon his theoretical positions and treatment approaches in Europe and the United States until his death in 1936. Today, individual psychology is a prominent tradition in the human services field with society members and supporters around the world.[6]

Although first memories have been an intense subject of research since the initial study on the topic in 1894, Adler was the first theorist to recognize the significant value of early recollections for under-standing the fundamental personality of a person and for gaining an insight into her outlook in life. He thought that first remembrances were unique for each individual and provide a known and tested pat-tern from which to navigate the future. Adler writes, "There are no 'chance memories': Out of the incalculable number of impressions which meet an individual, he chooses to remember only those which he feels, however darkly, to have a bearing on his situation. Thus, his memories represent his 'Story of My Life'; a story he repeats to himself to warn him or comfort him, to keep him concentrated on his goal, to prepare him, by means of past experiences, to meet the future with an already tested style of action."[7] Adler's perspective also suggests the varying purposes of early memories depending on the unique experiencing and motivation of people.

In a broader context, first memories relate to other primary con-cepts in Adler's theoretical orientation involving human behavior. In this regard, various principles from individual psychology contrib-ute to understanding the conceptual range and applications of early recollections from a broader perspective among diverse populations. Such concepts as lifestyle, degree of activity, and holism provide a framework for illuminating the meaning of first memories in a therapeutic context and in life. Although some of Adler's concepts may be less familiar to many people, he did attempt to describe them through terminology that would be understandable in their everyday lives.

## PURPOSEFULNESS OF EARLY RECOLLECTIONS

When Adler made the assertion that there are no indifferent or non-sensical early recollections, he gave prominence to the assumption that there is a *purposefulness* of the memories for an individual, which reflects an orientation to a way of being.[8] According to Adler, understanding a first remembrance involves clarifying the goal or goals that are integral to a person's memory. In this respect, the relatively few memories that are possible to recall from early childhood provide a guide or an orientation to an individual for present and future actions. There is a utility to first remembrances that can be emotionally stabilizing for a person because the memories convey a sense of what is intimately known about the world and how it seems to work. Through indelible impressions derived from first memories, an individual appears to develop a model or a prototype of what life is like or about. Acting upon these long-term convictions, a logical direction for a person to pursue are goals that are compatible with perceived conditions of existence. At the same time, just as the significance of the meaning of early memories is unfamiliar to most persons, the goal-directed nature of the memories is also largely unknown.

An individual's goal orientation relates to how he construes and makes sense of the world, and there are countless variations on this purposeful process. Some persons, for example, view life in positive and hopeful ways; others perceive existence as rather burdensome and dismal. In an important way, a person's outlook on life is unique and reflects the qualitative nature of his ingrained perspectives. Relating to the functional nature of early recollections, Adler writes, "They are not fortuitous phenomena, but speak clearly the language of encouragement or of warning."[9] To this point, for instance, consider the encouraging quality of a particular individual's first remembrance: "I was learning how to ride a bicycle and my mother was holding onto the seat while I tried to ride the bike. When I seemed to be riding okay, she let go, and I rode alone for a minute or so. It was fun, and I felt proud of myself." The language of encouragement in this memory conveys to the individual: "You are capable and have support." In a contrasting example, another person relates an early recollection involving a warning: "I was trying to ride a bicycle and was having a hard time keeping my balance. I fell off of the bike and hurt my knee. My father came out and started yelling at me, and I got up and ran behind the barn." The language of discouragement in this remembrance is: "Don't try things on your own because you are not capable."

## LIFESTYLE AND EARLY RECOLLECTIONS

In contemporary usage, the term *lifestyle* connotes something about how a person conducts or experiences life through visible and enduring patterns of behavior. Individuals exhibit lifestyles that are "rich," "healthy," "destructive," or other behavioral designations. In the media, various commercials connect an exciting lifestyle with the purchase of a new racy automobile or taking an exotic boat cruise. Yet, when Adler coined the terms *style of life* or *lifestyle* in the 1920s, he had in mind a broader and more profound concept in comparison to its current colloquial use.[10]

In Adler's view, an individual acquires fundamental assumptions about life that crystallize in early childhood during the first four or five years. This formation of the lifestyle encompasses unique formulations of a person's core beliefs toward oneself, other people, and events in life. In turn, the lifestyle functions as a unifying and goal-directed guide in the expression of an individual's behavior. The lifestyle enables a person to understand and forecast the nature of experiences through a familiar and tested means. Individuals see or perceive the world or the nature of experiences through the "lenses" of the lifestyle. For example, Alice, a thirty-year-old teacher, maintains core beliefs by which it is possible to formulate a lifestyle syllogism. "I am competent," "Other people are encouraging," "Events are stimulating," and therefore, "Life is fulfilling." When Alice finds herself in various situations, she generally feels capable of managing matters successfully and anticipates that other people likely will be supportive. As a result, events or experiences are usually interesting and enjoyable for Alice. In Adler's view, the ingrained convictions about existence set in early childhood remain largely stable over the life span. Change from a faulty or self-defeating lifestyle is possible, but initially requires insight into its purpose and function and a subsequent determination to establish more adaptive perspectives.

In his treatment practice, Adler would routinely ask clients to recount early childhood memories, and he was the first theorist to recognize the significant therapeutic value of this assessment procedure. Adler found that to understand an individual's lifestyle, the interpretation of early recollections provided the most effective appraisal means available. In this regard, Adler states, "Early recollections have especial significance. To begin with, they show the style of life in its origins and in its simplest expressions."[11] Although Adler emphasized early recollections in treatment contexts, he also employed a variety of other assessment methods for comprehensively illuminating the lifestyle or a client's outlook on life. As instructive illustrations, Adler provided numerous case examples in his writings of the employment of early recollections and their central role in understanding individuals.[12]

In a counseling example, Adler discussed the case of a young adult male referred to him due to social adjustment problems and the absence of friends. The client's early recollection is, "lying in a cot, looking round at the wallpaper and curtains."[13] Adler thought that the brief memory reflected the social isolation of the man and his interest in visual activity to the possible exclusion of interpersonal experiences. In a behavioral pattern reflecting the meaning of his first memory, the client withdrew from people and found some degree of satisfaction in visual pursuits of a solitary type. Although Adler did not provide a lifestyle syllogism, suggesting one for the client is possible: "I am better off alone," "Others are disruptive and distressing," "Events are satisfying in a passive, visual way," and, therefore, "Life is tolerable when I can just look at things by myself." Over time, however, such convictions of life proved to be excessively narrow and unfulfilling, as the client became further withdrawn and discontented. In treatment, Adler attempted to revise the client's maladaptive convictions toward more purposeful and constructive perspectives.

## STRIVING FOR SUPERIORITY
## AND EARLY RECOLLECTIONS

From Adler's perspective, within each individual, there is an inherent tendency toward growth and development that he referred to as *striving for superiority*. From an inferior to a superior position of development, persons strive to fulfill themselves through a fundamental motivational process.[14] This quest for self-realization is unique for each individual and has a potential to be adaptive or maladaptive. The striving is adaptive to the extent that the process involves an active pursuit of socially constructive endeavors, and assumes maladaptive or socially inappropriate dimensions when a person functions in a highly self-centered, excessively passive, or destructive way. In an illustration of the concept of striving for superiority, two individuals seek a goal of significance in life or a sense that they matter in the world. Alice finds a sense of significance as a young adult, by being a contributing and loving member of her family and community. In contrast, Albert pursues significance by dominating other people through demands for attention and service. Although both persons derive meaning from the same general intent of a quest for significance, their behavioral expressions are markedly different.

Adler found that early recollections have the potential to clarify the nature of an individual's striving for superiority.[15] To continue with the case examples from the previous section, Alice recalls the following first memory: "I was at the beach with my family, and we were sitting on a soft blanket near the water. I wanted to hold my baby brother, and asked my mother if I could. I had never held him before all by myself, and my mother placed him next to me. It felt so good to be able to hold him for a little while." The connection between Alice's striving for superiority through a socially useful means is evident in this memory. In a contrasting early remembrance, Albert relates: "I remember being at the grocery store with my mother. When we were checking out at the cash register, I saw all of this candy in front of me. My mother said that she wouldn't buy me any, and I started crying and screaming because I wanted some candy. At that point, she bought me a candy bar. I felt real happy when I got what I wanted." In this memory, Albert strives for superiority or significance by manipulating or using other people to his own advantage. As reflected in both early recollections, both Alice and Albert seek particular goals of superiority through active means. However, the direction of their striving differs considerably in terms of self-centeredness and cooperation with others. Adler recognized the essential quality of this particular dynamic through the use of the term "social interest."

## SOCIAL INTEREST AND EARLY RECOLLECTIONS

*Social interest* involves a sense of belonging and identification with other people and a desire to cooperate and contribute to the lives of others.[16] The capacity of social interest relates to an individual's ability to experience empathy and develop emotional ties through an affinity with other people.[17] A lack of social interest entails self-absorbed functioning and a disregard for the concerns and cares of others. Persons with low levels of social interest often strive for superiority at the expense of other people and tend to be more fearful and unhappy. Fostering the development of an individual's social interest in childhood and adolescence is enhanced through a nurturing and encouraging environment. Harsh and neglectful conditions in these key developmental periods often give rise to feelings of inferiority and hinder the growth of a person's social interest in more purposeful directions.

Early recollections frequently provide a means to recognize the relative degree of social interest in an individual's patterns of life.[18] Psychologically healthy individuals tend to engage their capacity for social interest in constructive and sustaining relationships with others. Adler also thought that it even was possible for people in an ever larger community to identify or empathize with "things which are quite outside our own body," such as animals an inanimate objects.[19]

This further reach of social interest is evident in the following first memory. As a young adult, Heather recalls: "I remember being six or seven years old. It was spring time, and it had just rained and the sun was coming out. My cousin asked me and my sister if we wanted to go outside to see something cool. We went outside and found these slugs under a stone. I remember my cousin poured salt on one of the slugs and it started dying. My sister and cousin just looked at what was going on, but I felt really bad for the slug because it was suffering. I got upset and started crying, and I was really mad at them for thinking it was cool."

Social interest encompasses a cooperative and compassionate intent on the part of an individual. Yet, as in Heather's first memory, the construct does not merely imply compliance or conformity. From Adler's view, social interest also involves nurturance and courage in order to advance to a purposeful or useful side of life. In the absence of social interest, there is a lack of empathic attunement and insensitivity to the joys or sorrows of others. In another example, consider the expression of social interest of Harry in his early recollection: "I remember waiting for Jimmy to come out of his house in the morning before school. When he got to the sidewalk I began to pound on him. He didn't even try to fight back. His nerdy glasses fell on the sidewalk, and I stepped on them with my foot. It felt so good to crush the glasses and see Jimmy cry like a baby." In his first memory, Harry appears to gain a sense of superiority through antisocial activity, while manifesting a low level of social interest.

## DEGREE OF ACTIVITY AND EARLY RECOLLECTIONS

Adler observed that individuals demonstrate varying patterns of initiative and engagement in life in forms of personal expression that he referred to as *degree of activity*.[20] On one end of an active/passive continuum, activity includes such functions as exercising capacities and skills, pursuing social involvements, and experiencing vivid

emotions. On the other end of the continuum, passivity entails inertness, withdrawal from social contact, and apathy or indifference.[21]
Adler believed that a significant measure of mental health relates to
an individual's pattern of active engagement in various tasks and
challenges in life. In a constructive direction when coupled with
social interest, people actively participate with others in cooperative
and contributing endeavors. In contrast, individuals possibly submit
to passive patterns of behavior because they feel deficient in striving
toward more communal or participatory functions.

A person with an active orientation typically demonstrates initiative, persistence, and engagement in experiences of life. In contrast
with a passive orientation, an individual gravitates toward evasive
behavior or a disengagement from various events. Adler thought that
the degree of activity of a person is acquired in early childhood and
remains relatively constant throughout life without an insight into
the pattern and a determination to change.[22] He also believed that it
is possible to detect an individual's degree of activity trends through
his early recollections.[23] As an example, Andrew, in early adulthood,
recounts an early memory, "I was about five years old and my father
and I were fishing out on a lake. He showed me how to put the bait
on the line and cast it out into the water. It was fun to be with him
and we were laughing a lot." In this memory, Andrew's heightened
degree of activity is evident along with a focus on social interest.
In a contrasting early recollection Joan, also in early adulthood,
relates, "I was lying down on my bed looking at the ceiling. I didn't
feel like doing anything. I remember my brother was playing on the
other side of the room." Joan's passive level of activity is apparent,
including a low engagement of social interest.

## HOLISM AND EARLY RECOLLECTIONS

In Adler's view, recognizing the dynamic unity or holistic quality
of an individual's behavior contributes to a greater understanding

of her lifestyle or outlook on life.[24] As an individual strives for superiority through specific goals, there is unity in behavior that Adler made reference to as *holism*. In this regard, individuals seem to function as an integrated whole in their feelings, beliefs, and actions. This assumption, however, raises questions because people often appear to act in inconsistent and mixed up ways. Yet, an intentionality or purpose operates in a consistent manner that becomes observable as a person reacts to various situations. As an example, Bill, a thirty-year-old carpenter, seems unable to decide if he should pursue a long-term relationship with Edith. He appears emotionally torn between his affection toward Edith and does not appear able to make up his mind about making a serious commitment. Yet, when considering this apparent conflict holistically, there is a pattern to Bill's behavior: he does not wish to become involved in an extended relationship. Bill seems hesitant and inconsistent, but there is a consistency in his avoidance functioning that defers his decision to sometime in the future. In this regard, Adler made the point that it is possible to weave all details of an individual's personality together to see the whole in the details.[25] To continue with the case of Bill, he decides to avoid communicating with Edith for several days. This action would appear to jeopardize his emotional ties with her, but it is in accord with his intention to avoid a long-term relationship.

Relating the principle of holism to first memories of the countless experiences that individuals are exposed to in early childhood, only events that relate to their outlook on life seem to be remembered. If this assumption is accurate, there should be a correspondence in first memories that reflect the unity of an individual's personality and way of being. Rudolph Dreikurs, a prominent associate of Alfred Adler, endorsed this point by stating, "All early recollections show, therefore, the same pattern; where they differ, they supplement but never contradict each other."[26] Employing this line of reasoning, integrating two or more first remembrances contributes to a more expansive and holistic way of knowing a person. As an example, recall Heather's early recollection in the previous section involving the slugs and how upset she became over their treatment. With this memory in mind, consider another first memory of Heather's: "I can remember being around six or seven, sitting in my room at my old house playing dolls with my sister. We would set up the whole room as if it were a town and could play all day. I liked dressing them up and playing with their hair." Although the two memories involve markedly different events, there is compatibility in the recollections. In both remembrances, Heather demonstrates a clear level of social interest through a caring response to the slugs and toward her dolls. A coherent pattern emerges in both memories as Heather is active and shows initiative in cooperative and participatory endeavors. As an expression of social interest, the memory with the slugs suggests that Heather is willing to relinquish her calm and peaceful existence to speak out for the defenseless.

## FAMILY CONSTELLATION
## AND EARLY RECOLLECTIONS

Another major principle of individual psychology involves Adler's emphasis on birth order within families and the relationship that it has with an individual's characteristic personality features. Although Adler stated that birth order suggests tendencies only in terms of accuracy, ordinal positioning has gained broad interest among practitioners and the general public.[27] Birth order comprises five respective positions within a family: oldest, second, middle, youngest, and only child. In a brief profile of personality characteristics relating to birth order: firstborn children show a trend to achieve more than later borns, second or middle children may be ambitious and try to surpass the older sibling, and the last or youngest child has a need to know that he is appreciated. Beyond birth order, the family constellation encompasses the functioning of each parent, values and traditions, and patterns of discipline, affection, and communication.

With respect to early recollections, implications pertaining to the family constellation may occasionally emerge in a person's remembrances. In particular, evaluating an individual's relationship with specific family members is sometimes possible through a first memory. As an example, Justin, as the oldest child in the family, relates an early memory: "I was visiting my aunt's house with my parents and my baby brother who was a new baby. When we got to the front door of the house, there were a lot of people there, and everyone was so excited to see my brother. Nobody bothered with me and I felt ignored. It was like I was not important." In this remembrance, Justin appears to be dethroned from a position of significance as the oldest child. At the same time, many early memories do not include family members, and making inferences that involve the family constellation are not feasible. Importantly, in early recollections the identifiable people often represent prototypes of individuals in a general sense. In Justin's case, for instance, he feels resentful toward the adult family members for overlooking him and also generalizes these feelings to many individuals whom he encounters in life.

Since the period of Adler's innovative work, numerous researchers have made contributions for advancing an understanding of first memories. In the next four chapters, Part II of the text builds on this wide-ranging scholarship for clarifying the meaning and implications of early recollections through the *Dawn of Memories* model.

## Part II

# INTERPRETATION AND MEANINGS OF EARLY RECOLLECTIONS

## Chapter Four

# Life Is What I First Recall

## *The Interpretation and Meaning of Early Recollections*

The important things are what we remember after we have forgotten everything else.

—Virginia Axline[1]

At the heart of interpreting the meaning of early recollections are the intriguing questions of why people recall particular memories, and why do they remember them in certain ways?[2] Of the innumerable experiences in which children engage during their first seven years of life, they are usually only able to call to mind a handful of memories from this developmental period.[3] From a total spontaneous recall that typically ranges in single digits, a reasonable assumption is that each individual memory conveys a special meaning for an individual. With respect to the question of why people retain particular memories from early childhood, Alfred Adler was the first theorist to recognize that early memories have the potential to reveal basic and compelling ways that people perceive life.[4] Importantly, this method of making inferences from the first remembrances rests on the critical assumption that the content or topics evoked in a person's early recollections convey fundamental aspects of her psychological functioning. As a consequence, the possibility exists for translating particular features of first memories into characteristic thought processes and behavioral patterns of individuals, which provides support for the viability of Adler's approach.

# PERSONALITY APPRAISAL
## AND EARLY RECOLLECTIONS

When considering the use of early recollections as a personality assessment tool, a crucial question arises relating to how stable or enduring the remembrances are in a person's life over an extended period of time. If the memories change depending on transient and variable states in the life of a person, they are not particularly helpful or reliable for evaluating personality characteristics and ways of being. On the other hand, if recollections from the first years of childhood are generally persistent over the life course, they offer a promise for assessing ingrained aspects of personality functioning. As an example, a forty-year-old man relates an early recollection about joyfully riding a bicycle for the first time on a summer day. Is this particular memory a product of the individual's pleasant mood at the time he recalls the memory, or does the recollection reflect a trend toward an optimistic pattern of life? In an attempt to clarify this important "state versus trait" question, several researchers have given consideration to the stability or enduring quality of early memories in various investigations.[5] In a long-term or longitudinal study, Ruthellen Josselson, a faculty member with The Fielding Institute and a professor of psychology at the Hebrew University of Jerusalem, asked twenty-four randomly selected female college students to recall their early memories on three separate occasions over a twenty-two-year period.[6] In analyzing the results of her study, Josselson found that the first remembrances of the women were largely stable in terms of thematic content, with very subtle changes, for more than two decades of life. Consistent with Josselson's findings, when recalling my early recollections today, they evoke visual scenes and emotional reactions similar to those that came to mind when I first began to evaluate the remembrances some forty years ago.

In what is referred to as a *projective technique*, early recollections belong to a collection of personality assessment instruments with a lengthy and controversial history in counseling and psychology.[7]

With its origin in the 1920s, the Rorschach Ink Blot Test is the most famous projective appraisal device in the world.[8] In this assessment procedure, individuals describe what they see on ten ambiguous stimulus cards presented to them. Similar to the Rorschach and other projective approaches, early recollections utilize brief, general instructions: "Think back to a long time ago when you were little, and try to recall one of your first memories, one of the first things that you can remember."[9] Early recollections also involve a relatively unstructured task of eliciting memories from the early childhood stage before a person is eight years old. As with some other projective techniques, an individual's disclosures of first memories yield a virtually unlimited range of unique responses relating to the content of the remembrances. Through an interpretation process, the material generated from early recollection responses provide insights into the lifestyle or ingrained outlook on life of a person. At the same time, most people are unaware that their initial childhood memories have a potential to reveal a rich source of personal understanding relating to their ways of being and patterns of life.

Similar to the features of most other projective techniques, the same qualities that may be seen as strengths in the employment of early recollections as a personality assessment tool also represent potential weaknesses. The incalculable number of human responses, which are possible to evoke relating to a simple question about first remembrances, creates major challenges in interpreting their meanings with accuracy. Collectively, human beings are capable of recalling an infinite variety in the content of early childhood experiences in all sorts of contexts. Attempting to evaluate first memories among groups of individuals by establishing norms or standards of usage can produce vast and daunting amounts of data. Even with the contemporary availability of statistical computations, an empirical analysis for interpreting early recollections has not been viable because each remembrance is a unique and one-time construction of a person. At the same time however, a number of researchers have attempted to develop early recollection interpretation systems since Adler first discovered the therapeutic value of understanding.

# EARLY RECOLLECTIONS INTERPRETATION
# APPROACH OF ALFRED ADLER

With his capacity to intuitively and artistically elicit and interpret first memories, Adler found the remembrances to yield the most important means for understanding the style of life of individuals better than any other assessment procedure at his disposal.[10] Adler had an exceptional ability to empathize with people and creatively employ early childhood memories to understand how individuals experience and perceive their world. Unfortunately, however, Adler did not systematically discuss in his writings how he was able to intuitively grasp a range of human personality dimensions and patterns of behavior in utilizing first memories in a treatment context or in everyday life. At the same time, Adler wrote several works featuring early recollections, and these writings are available for gleaning clues for interpreting the remembrances.[11] Adler made reference to numerous case studies of patients or clients, including impressionistic commentary on his treatment approach when interpreting first memories. In a particular case, a young man recalls an early memory: "I was running round the whole day in a kiddy car."[12] From this brief remembrance, Adler recognized as a central emphasis the individual's orientation to movement and motor activities. Among various issues confronting the client, he was having difficulty adjusting to sedentary occupations in his life. In a rather humorous conclusion to the case, the young man eventually found compatible and enjoyable employment as a traveling salesman!

Perhaps the most prominent and critical aspect of Adler's early recollection interpretation method involved distinguishing themes or the central idea of an individual's memories. With reference to the previous kiddy car remembrance, movement in the form of a mobile activity represents a compelling focus and provides a basic thematic structure or a "big picture" relating to the individual's memory. Identifying a theme relates to the brief story that is happening in a remembrance, and researchers after Adler consistently used a thematic analysis in formulating early memory interpretation approaches and procedures.[13]

Beyond pointing to the centrality of themes, Adler and subsequent researchers began to focus on the identification of various personality traits and dimensions in their development of interpretation methods for first memories. Adler initiated this practice by giving consideration to such personality facets as social interest and the degree of activity of individuals which were detectable in their early recollections.[14] As an example, as a young adult, Sarah recalls a memory when she was a young girl. Sarah was trying to tie her shoelaces, and her mother was standing nearby encouraging her to complete the task. Sarah successfully tied her shoes and felt proud of her accomplishment. In this remembrance, Sarah's constructive persistence in working at the task and positive interactions with her mother suggests the personality dimensions of a high level of activity and social interest.

## EARLY RECOLLECTIONS INTERPRETATION METHODS

Various researchers after Adler investigated a range of personality dimensions relating to early recollections, and they followed the convention of detecting the presence or relative absence of the human qualities in the memories of diverse populations, including normal and abnormal categorizations. The interpretation or scoring approaches of the remembrances developed by the researchers began to utilize the assignment of an individual's responses to predetermined categories of personality and other aspects of functioning. In the most widely used early recollection interpretation research instrument, Guy Manaster, a professor at the University of Texas at Austin, and Thomas Perryman, a professor at San Jacinto College, devised a scoring model involving seven categories.[15] The main personality variables of the Manaster-Perryman system included the active-passive dimension and the internal-external locus of control of a person. Locus of control relates to how much influence people feel that they have in directing the outcome of their lives in positive and negative directions. People with an external locus of control tend to believe that life outcomes are largely outside their influence, and those with an internal locus of control behave in a way that they can affect change through their personal efforts. In an early recollection example of external locus of control, Darlene recalls a memory taking place in the first grade. "I remember the teacher asking me to draw something on the blackboard. Most of the other kids had already gone up to write on the board, but I didn't think that I could do it. I stayed in my seat and felt embarrassed." In contrast to Darlene's demonstration of external locus of control as it relates to her recollection, a classmate, Ellen, experiences an internal locus of control. Under similar circumstances, Ellen remembers eagerly going to the front of the class, feeling confident in her ability to write something on the blackboard.

Manaster and Perryman provided other insightful ways of evaluating early recollections with their emphasis on giving consideration to sensory modalities and the setting or location of the memories. In their research, Manaster and Perryman found that the visual function was overwhelmingly evident in the accounts of individuals' first memories, and the representation of any of the five senses was thought to be implicated in an individual's sensory preferences in life. The location in a first memory is unique to a person, and its emphasis, according to the researchers, suggested his valuation of a particular setting. As an example, relating to Manaster and Perryman's research findings, the following early recollection emphasizes the sense of touch of an individual and the specific setting or place of her memory. As a thirty-five-year-old, Joyce recalls, "I remember sitting on a white chair in my bedroom and my mother was combing my hair. She's putting my strands of hair in braids, and it is such a good and comforting feeling. Her hands were soft and gentle as she touches my hair and head. My room was a nice blue color, and I'm wrapped in a warm comforter." In this remembrance touch is a significant modality for Joyce and home and her bedroom are special places that convey an alluring appeal. Joyce's caring relationship with her mother is also evident in the memory. Throughout her life, Joyce has been particularly sensitive to the modality of touch. In such areas as the warmth and softness of clothing and Joyce's desire to receive frequent touch in intimate relationships, touch is a prominent and influential sense. Relating to settings or place, Joyce finds that her bedroom and the rest of her home provide a sense of well-being, and "coming home" always has a beckoning quality. Home for Joyce is also associated with loving feelings that she has for her mother.

In my review of modes of perception beyond the senses and place, two other variables consistently have appeared in the research literature relating to early recollections and in the remembrances of individuals with whom I had contact: color and physical objects. With respect to the perception of color, Thomas Sweeney and Jane Myers, professors at the University of North Carolina at Greensboro, found that only a minority of people depict events in color in their first memories and the majority of people "see" their remembrances in black and white.[16] The individuals who observe the presence of color in their remembrances make such statements as "The sky is blue," or "The sun's rays are shining through the window." In the view of Sweeney and Myers, people with color representation in early childhood memories often have an affinity with color in their lives. This may appear in such behavioral expressions as discriminating choices of color of attire, an emphasis and attention to color coordination in home décor, and an appreciation of color in various aspects of life. As another perceptual modality, the physical presence of objects is a prominent focus of attention to some individuals in early recollections, and with other people objects are more of a secondary or incidental nature.[17] When distinct objects in first memories are notable and evoke emotional reactions, they often have a special meaning to people in their lives. For example, in the first remembrance of Albert Einstein, his father showed him a compass, and Einstein was fascinated by the magnetic workings of the instrument that he held

in his hands.[18] In Einstein's life, scientific objects provided essential
problem-solving functions in his research, and his theorizing about
objects on a physical plane made him a world-renowned physicist.


## DAWN OF MEMORIES, AN EARLY
## RECOLLECTIONS INTERPRETATION MODEL

In formulating a new approach to the interpretation of the meaning
of early recollections, I drew together essential elements from major
scoring approaches that have been published since Adler's initial
work with first memories. Given that themes and thematic analysis
were present in all of the early memory interpretation systems that
I reviewed, an analysis of themes assumed a major role in my interpretation model. Attempting to grasp the central idea or core ideas of
an individual's first memories affords a prominent focus to themes
as they relate to the ways of being of people. Attention to various
personality dimensions was another primary emphasis across the
scoring systems in my review. In selecting personality variables for
inclusion, particular qualities are critical for clarifying the meaning
of early recollections and for their psychological implications in life.
I chose to include the following personality dimensions in my early
recollection interpretive method: degree of activity, social interest,
optimistic/pessimistic, self-efficacy, and conscientiousness. Finally,
particular modes of perception are detectable in early recollections
and contribute to grasping the way of being of people in the broad
context of their lives. My selection of the perceptual modalities include: senses, color, place or location, and physical objects. The next
chapter provides an overview of the *Dawn of Memories, An Early
Recollections Interpretation* model by evaluating a first childhood
memory of Benjamin Franklin as it relates to his life in eighteenth-
century colonial America.

## Chapter Five

# "The Whistle"

## *Dawn of Memories, An Early Recollections Interpretation Model*

Our earliest childhood memories have a magical quality about them, if for no other reason than their being the apparent beginning of our conscious lives.

—Patrick Huyghe[1]

Beyond his prominent role as a Founding Father of his country, Benjamin Franklin made numerous contributions to humanity throughout his life as a writer, scientist, inventor, statesman, diplomat, and philanthropist. Yet, what may be most memorable about Franklin is the iconic image of him flying a kite in a thunderstorm to prove that lightning has an electric current. His serene face and shoulder-length hair are universally familiar as an eminent historical figure in colonial America. In Franklin's celebrated *Autobiography*, he narrated a detailed account of his long and fruitful life as well as his influence in shaping the growth and values of a new nation.[2] In another composition, "The Whistle," written in his old age, Franklin recounted an early memory that provides a resource for revealing features of his personality and what was most meaningful to him in life.[3] The scope and complexity of the recollection is exemplary for demonstrating the interpretation process of early memories. After profiling an account of Franklin's life, my discussion focuses on interpreting his early childhood remembrance through the *Dawn of Memories* model.

## THE LIFE OF BENJAMIN FRANKLIN

Benjamin Franklin was born in Boston in 1706, as the fifteenth of seventeen children. Although his formal education ended after only a few years, his pursuit of knowledge and a quest for personal development was insatiable. At the age of seventeen, with a meager amount of money in his pocket, Franklin left Boston and traveled to Philadelphia and found work as a printer's apprentice.[4] Through his diligence, fondness for words, and self-taught skill as a writer, Franklin flourished in the printing business, achieving success in newspaper publishing and book dealing. In 1732 Franklin began to produce a series of almanacs entitled *Poor Richard's Almanack*.[5] The editions contained a wry mix of humor, moral admonitions, and pragmatic information that was especially popular in the expanding colonial nation. While extolling such virtues as industry and frugality, Franklin would offer maxims like, "He that is rich need not live sparingly, and he that can live sparingly need not be rich to live."[6] On a voyage to England in 1757, Franklin reviewed all of his almanacs from the previous twenty-five years in order to write *The Way of Wealth*, which, in addition to his *Autobiography*, was among his most famous works.[7]

His inherent tendency to problem-solve and high level of intellectual curiosity caused Franklin to find science and technology intensely appealing throughout his life. Most of his inventive thinking was directed toward finding practical solutions to problems of everyday existence. Discoveries with electricity and the invention of the lightning rod brought him international acclaim. Franklin's scientific inquiries and industriousness led to advances in the knowledge of meteorology, refrigeration, heating, and agriculture in the pursuit of useful ways to improve the lives of people. Furthermore, Franklin invented bifocal glasses, and his innovative design of the Franklin stove made heating more efficient. As Franklin's reputation grew as a premier scientist, his views and opinions became widely known and sought out in the colonies and across Europe. Franklin also perfected a new musical instrument, the glass armonica, which produced a resonant tone by rubbing a wet finger around the rims of different sized glass vessels.[8]

At the early age of forty-two, Franklin retired from his prosperous printing businesses and dedicated himself to public service through a variety of ambitious civic endeavors. To enhance the safety and security of the citizens of Philadelphia, Franklin played an instrumental role in giving birth to a property insurance company, firefighting corps, lending library, hospital, militia, university, learned society, and other community improvements.[9] In 1753, Franklin was appointed to the position of deputy postmaster general of North America and immediately began to expand postal services and make the widespread operations more efficient. With his unpretentious demeanor and convivial humor, Franklin became the most active member of the Pennsylvania Assembly and assumed an outspoken role in criticizing England's policies toward colonial America.[10] Franklin was elected to the office of president of Pennsylvania, and in 1775 he took a seat in the First Continental Congress where he joined a small committee to compose the Declaration of Independence.

In the final stage of his remarkable life, Franklin's name became even more celebrated internationally due to his diplomatic success as an ambassador in France in addition to his congressional appointment in 1781 as a commissioner charged with negotiating peace with England on behalf of the United States. With his health failing, Franklin served as the oldest member of the Constitutional Convention in one of his last acts to advance the common good. In 1790, at the age of eighty-four, Franklin died and was buried in the cemetery of Christ Church in Philadelphia beside his wife, Deborah, and son, Francis.[11]

## AN EARLY RECOLLECTION OF BENJAMIN FRANKLIN

On November 10, 1779, in a correspondence to his friend Madame Brillion, of Passy, France, Franklin wrote "The Whistle." Written while he lived in Passy, this short essay or bagatelle recounted Franklin's early childhood memory:

> When I was a child of seven years old, my friends, on a holiday, filled my pockets with coppers. I went directly to a shop where they sold toys for children; and, being charmed with the sound of a whistle that I met by the way in the hands of another boy; I voluntarily offered and gave all of my money for one. I then came home, and went whistling all over the house, much pleased with my whistle, but disturbing all the family. My brothers and sisters and cousins, understanding the bargain I had made, told me I had given four times as much for it as it was worth; put me in mind what good things I might have bought with the rest of the money; and laughed at me so much for my folly that I cried with vexation; and the reflection gave me more chagrin than the whistle gave me pleasure.[12]

## AN INTERPRETATION OF
## BENJAMIN FRANKLIN'S EARLY RECOLLECTION

Using the *Dawn of Memories* model, the interpretation of early childhood memories involves three levels or perspectives: core themes, personality dimensions, and perceptual modalities. Thematically, an initial focus attempts to discern the main topic or the essential point of the memory. With respect to Franklin's remembrance, this pursuit seeks to grasp the central idea or the "big picture" of his early recollection. Relating to personality dimensions, analysis shifts to evaluating the meaning of key personality variables, which are detectable in a remembrance, such as degree of activity and conscientiousness. Through the narration of Franklin's first memory, consideration is given to each of five critical characteristics to determine their qualitative emphasis in his life. In the last interpretive phase, attention turns to the use of early recollections for evaluating an individual's perceptual modalities and ways of perceiving the world. Judgments are made relating to the orientating influence on Franklin's experience in each of the modes that includes the five senses, color, place, and objects. Although the appraisal process emphasizes the three perspectives separately, there is unity to an individual's personality functioning or lifestyle. This holistic pattern should become recognizable through an interpretation of Franklin's first remembrance in the context of his remarkable life.

## Core Theme

A key aspect for understanding the meaning of early recollections is the function of empathy.[13] When listening to an individual's verbal recounting or reading the narrative version of a first memory, it is possible to experience for a fleeting period what it is like to be the person relating the remembrance. Human beings have an empathic capacity to evoke visual and other sensory images when attuning to an individual's early childhood memory. In reference to a thematic analysis in early recollections, identifying the basic plot or topic of the event is a primary focus. In much the same way that theme parks ("The Future" and "The Wild West") connect amusement activities in an overall way, a core theme is detectable in the narration of a first remembrance, which provides a central connecting idea. As in a brief story, the theme conveys the main point of the narrative or what is going on.

From a thematic perspective, the core theme of Franklin's early recollection seems to relate to a "lesson learned."[14] As bitter as it was for Franklin to realize and admit his error, his emotional response suggests a determination to learn from his jarring mistake. In this sense, the theme extends from an awareness of the misjudgment to a resolve to do better in his life. Franklin captures this sentiment in *Poor Richard's Almanack*, "The things which hurt, instruct."[15] The nature of the hard lesson also implies that to restrain impulsive and wasteful actions, employing a measure of prudence and reason is critical. As Franklin seemed to learn, rectifying or finding solutions to problems is more likely to occur by seeking practical, rather than frivolous, outcomes. As in his early recollection, this appears to involve listening to others, including what is unpleasant or even hard to hear, and adapting to changing conditions.

Various aspects of the core theme of a lesson learned are recognizable over the course of Franklin's immensely productive life. In "The Whistle" Franklin made the point that most troubles and miseries of life are brought by people upon themselves "by the false estimates they have made of the value of things and by their *giving too much for their whistles.*"[16] In his *Autobiography*, a repetitive pattern in his commentaries involves Franklin making or acknowledging mistakes and then making amends for his errors and shortcomings.[17] As an example, Franklin paid scant attention to a young woman named Deborah Read in a chance meeting with her upon arriving in Philadelphia as a youth. Years later recognizing his mistreatment and oversight, he began to court Deborah, and they were married in 1730.[18] Franklin's determination to improve himself was evident as he resourcefully sought to develop his writing skills, proficiency in foreign languages, and moral behavior. In *Poor Richard's Almanack*, the *Autobiography*, and other literary works, he emphasized principles of prudence and reason so that people might avoid waste, and live useful and productive lives. His quest to find solutions to problems of everyday life led to practical inventions as well as his discoveries in science and technology. As in his early recollection, Franklin demonstrated an inherent tendency to listen to others and learn from them. Adaptation to change became a way of life for Franklin. In the pursuit of new and challenging experiences, for example, on several occasions he relinquished stable and lucrative positions in search of emerging business and political opportunities.

## Personality Dimensions

In the vast literature on personality and human behavior, certain qualities constitute key variables in portraying the uniqueness of an individual. Early recollections contribute to clarifying distinctive aspects of a person's enduring patterns of functioning and way of being. Identifying the various dimensions of personality that emerge when evaluating first memories makes it possible to select particular characteristics that have implications for an individual's mental health and emotional well-being. These variables are also prominent in the research on early recollections, and are potentially subject to change and development. My choice of personality dimensions for the *Dawn of Memories* model include: degree of activity, social interest, optimistic/pessimistic, self-efficacy, and conscientiousness. Discussing the variables in the context of Benjamin Franklin's life brings clarity to each personality dimension.

## Degree of Activity

As a personality dimension, degree of activity relates to an individual's pattern of initiative and engagement in the experiences and tasks in life.[19] Higher levels of activity are associated with attempts to seek out various endeavors and ventures in a purposeful and persistent way. Typically, more intense activity involves elevations in emotional response and a commitment to a range of functions and pursuits. In contrast, a person manifesting a low degree of activity assumes a passive way of being including patterns of stagnation, inertness, and withdrawal. The individual typically seeks to avoid challenges and adversities in life. This behavior will often result in emotional reactions that include feelings of apathy, dispassion, and indifference.

The high degree of activity of Ben Franklin was continuous from his venturesome days as a youth on the streets of Boston to the end of his energetic life as a world-renowned figure. Franklin was highly active and mobile in his early recollection and in his life. He was constantly on the move through travels and personal explorations that took him throughout Europe and many parts of colonial America.[20] His engagement of activity, however, went far beyond the physical and geographical realms to include social, intellectual, entrepreneurial, moral, governmental, and scientific arenas. He had an unbounded level of interest in all things relating to the human condition, which was visible in his attendant ways of improving the lives of people. His energetic capacity to initiate creative endeavors and see them through to fruition was a way of life for Franklin. Similar to his early recollection, Franklin thrived in the role of being the center of attention and in seeking out things and people that provoked his curiosity and interest. He had a passion for living that found expression through a strong degree of activity in sustaining purposeful experiences.

*Social Interest*

As another essential personality variable, social interest pertains to an identification or an affinity with humanity.[21] A person with higher levels of social interest commonly evokes reactions of compassion and empathy toward other people and engages in cooperative activities that contribute to the welfare of others.[22] With an elevated social interest, an individual tends to experience both feelings of belonging within a community and an emotional bond with other people. The person potentially derives a sense of purpose or meaning in life and the enhancement of well-being through the pursuit of socially useful endeavors. In a contrasting direction, an individual with low levels of social interest frequently experiences patterns of emotional detachment or alienation from others. Typically, such a person maintains a preoccupation with oneself and a lack of compassion or empathy toward others.

Benjamin Franklin seemed to radiate a tolerance and acceptance of himself and others, as well as relish his role as a productive and prominent member of society. His social interest was high, and he constantly sought out ways to improve himself and enhance the personal condition of others. Franklin's strong desire to improve the daily lives of people was continuous over the course of his purposeful life. Whether it was through his practical inventions and experiments, civic-minded consciousness, or community improvement efforts, Franklin demonstrated a commitment to lead a socially useful existence. In this regard, in *Poor Richard's Almanack*, Franklin writes, "The noblest question in the world is *what good may I do in it?*"[23] Through Franklin's contributions to public-spirited projects such as schools, hospitals, and lending libraries, he advanced the betterment of society on numerous fronts. His written works were replete with hints and admonitions on how to live a life of virtue and benevolence. At the same time, Franklin had a wry self-awareness, and frequently acknowledged his limitations and failings. Through this lens it is possible to point to an aspect of Franklin's behavior which was characterized by excessively lengthy absences from his wife and children due to ambassadorial appointments and personal travels in England and France. Of course these patterns raise questions about his emotional commitment to his family.

## Optimism/Pessimism

As evaluative stances, optimism and pessimism relate to favorable or unfavorable expectations that individuals maintain about life.[24] Although optimism and pessimism are often considered categorically, there are variations within each dimension that range from high to low. In other words, it is possible for a person to maintain a strong or weak trend of either optimism or pessimism. An individual with an optimistic outlook frequently experiences feelings of contentment and satisfaction with life and has positive expectations for the future.[25] Challenges and demands are typically faced by engaging in problem-focused activities, including the possibility of finding meaning in responding to adversities. The individual maintains a belief in his abilities to bring about desired change and outcomes. With a higher expectation for success, a persistent effort toward the achievement of goals is commonly found among those with an optimistic outlook on life. When threats occur to personal capabilities, the individual usually assumes responsibility for one's actions rather than blaming others or environmental conditions.

In a contrasting direction, a person with an ingrained pessimistic perspective frequently experiences feelings of discontentment and dissatisfaction with life and has negative expectations for the future. When faced with challenges and demands, disengagement from problem-focused activities is common. The person experiences doubts and uncertainties about his or her abilities to bring about favorable outcomes and change. With low expectations for success, minimal efforts are typically made toward the pursuit of goals. When threats to personal capabilities occur, avoiding responsibility for actions and blaming others or environmental conditions is a common pattern of the individual.

Benjamin Franklin's congenial approach to life involved strong measures of vitality, friendliness, good humor, sociability, and a way of being that conveyed a high level of optimism which found particular expression in interpersonal relationships and in his extensive writings. Franklin's favorable expectations for the future were integral to his belief in a person's potential for change and development. In Franklin's view, the possibility for individuals to strive to improve themselves and to learn from their mistakes provides hope for the future. Franklin approached human affairs with the conviction that things will usually work out for the best when persistent efforts are made to problem-solve and find solutions to challenges in living. Such pursuits are most often of a practical nature and are within the capacities of humankind to address. In his *Autobiography*, Franklin references this quest for happiness, "Human felicity is produced not so much by great pieces of good fortune that seldom happen, as by little advantages that occur every day."[26] Franklin had a strong belief in his own ability and the capabilities of others to initiate change and seek purposeful goals. Although he recognized the tendency of people to rationalize and avoid assuming responsibility when emotionally threatened, Franklin was tolerant of such human failings. At the same time, he spoke to the importance of facing difficulties and challenges more directly in order to lead a more satisfying and fulfilling life.

## Self-Efficacy

As a personality quality, self-efficacy relates to the personal belief of individuals who generally anticipate success in challenging situations.[27] Through feedback from others and environmental experiences, a person develops enduring perceptions of self-efficacy. Higher levels of self-efficacy involve a conviction of being able to manage or cope with stressful events. With a personal sense of efficacy, an individual feels motivated to persevere and exercise control over perceived obstacles. More positive self-efficacy also entails an increased regulation and control over cognitions or thoughts and a greater likelihood of maintaining composure in anxiety-provoking situations. An individual with higher levels of self-efficacy frequently demonstrates purposeful ways to reduce stress and make her environment less stressful. In contrast, a person with lower levels of self-efficacy maintains convictions of possessing only minimal abilities to cope with stressful events or overcome adversities. Obstacles are frequently perceived as beyond personal control and induce a desire to withdraw or give up. A lessened degree of efficacy often entails a diminishment in the regulation and control over thinking and an inability to maintain composure in anxiety-provoking situations. Typically, a person with low self-efficacy also fails to seek out strategies to reduce personal stress or make his environment more relaxing.

In Benjamin Franklin's early recollection, he received feedback from his family members that he had made a foolish blunder in purchasing the overpriced whistle. Although the comments were stinging, Franklin did not become defensive, and instead took the communication to heart as a lesson learned. Franklin's reaction suggests a high level of self-efficacy in his capacity to respond to and even embrace challenging situations. In this regard, Franklin demonstrated self-efficacy throughout his life in various endeavors and pursuits. Franklin was tenacious in his personal beliefs and confident about his ability to overcome obstacles. This degree of tenacity was evident with Franklin's years of devotion to intricate scientific experiments, prompting reluctant participants to join him in civil and public improvement projects, assuming demanding positions in the development of a national government, and contending with serious infirmities in the later years of his life. Within his family, Franklin hesitated to have his son, Francis, inoculated against smallpox because he was not feeling well at the time. Although Franklin publically supported inoculation efforts, Francis soon died due to smallpox at the age of four.[28] Franklin was distraught with grief over the loss and many years later commented about the importance of Francis in his life, referring to him as, "the apple of my eye."[29] Franklin frequently demonstrated an ability to manage stress in his own life, and he made significant strides in making his environment and the conditions of others less stressful. Innovations in heating and air conditioning, the lightning rod, a musical instrument, postal services, agriculture, opticals, safety and security procurements, and more contributed to making everyday life less demanding and more manageable. Franklin's resolutions and maxims in his writings emphasized the importance of restraining self-defeating human emotions and sagely using the capacity to reason. Franklin's level of industry and ability to work hard was tireless, reflecting a belief in his perceived ability to surmount challenges and adversities.

## Conscientiousness

As a personality dimension, conscientiousness encompasses a number of factors including diligent, persistent, productive, and responsible behavior.[30] A person with a high level of conscientiousness tends to follow a planful approach to tasks in addition to being well organized. An ability to delay gratification and to persist in the accomplishment of goals are aspects of conscientiousness that are commonly observed. Perseverance, orderliness, and behaving ethically are additional characteristics of a pattern of conscientiousness. In a contrasting direction, an individual with a low level of conscientiousness has a tendency to demonstrate indolent, unproductive, and irresponsible behavior. A minimal restraint or delay of gratification and a lack of persistence toward the accomplishment of goals are common trends. Other characteristic deficits in conscientiousness include hesitating or yielding in the face of difficulties, disregarding order in matters of everyday living, and behaving unethically.

Benjamin Franklin's sense of responsibility and a commitment to a productive life was strong. In his *Autobiography* Franklin wrote, "Waste neither Time nor Money, but make the best use of both."[31] His steady diligence was supported by a planful and well-organized way of life with a high expression of conscientiousness. Franklin had a capacity to delay gratification and persist with the pursuit and accomplishment of goals that were fundamental to his nature. As a young man, for instance, he became a vegetarian in order to save money which he would often use to buy books.[32] In another example of persistence, as a printer's apprentice, Franklin had access to books that he would borrow, read late into the night, and then return the following morning. Franklin made continuous reference in his writings to the importance of attempting to live a virtuous life. Although he would often acknowledge his shortcomings and failures in measuring up to ethical principles, this did not restrict his determination to make moral declarations. In his *Autobiography*, Franklin proposed a set of thirteen virtues, such as industry and sincerity, for himself and others to follow in an orderly way.[33] Bringing to mind the image of his early recollection, Franklin makes frugality a moral imperative by stating, "Make no Expense but to do good to others or yourself: i.e. waste nothing."[34]

## Perceptual Modalities

The five senses are human endowments that provide ways of knowing about the world and are unique to each individual in life.

Understanding patterns of how a person engages in life and makes meaning of sensory experiences provides glimpses into his personality functioning. When recounting an early childhood memory, an individual's narration invariably reveals particular sense expressions. In turn, the emphasis given to each sense in the remembrance contributes to empathically understanding the person. For most people, visual images are dominant in early recollections; representations of the other senses occur with far less frequency.[35] For many individuals who experience sound, touch, smell, or taste in their remembrances, these relatively rare sensory expressions tend to be orienting in their lives. As an example, a woman who reports instances of touch in her first memory experiences a sensitivity to touch that finds expression in a frequent desire to be touched in intimate relationships, and she has a heightened awareness to the smoothness of apparel textures on her body. In another direction, a person may make reference to the perceptions of color, place or location, or material objects in his early recollections. When people identify prominent and distinct rememberances in their images, the perceptions potentially assume a significant role and influence in the life of the individuals.

*Senses*

Describing an early recollection without bringing to mind visual images is impossible for most people. In recalling a remembrance, a person typically pictures oneself engaging in some type of activity. By far, most first memories are silent; when sounds do occur they are often in the context of conversations or a distinct noise in the environment. Touch is also rare as a sensory expression for an individual in early recollections and is most often expressed through human interactions or touching particular objects. Smell and taste materialize with even less frequency in the form of smelling or eating natural or man-made substances. For early recollection interpretation purposes, an emphasis will be given to each of the senses in a subsequent chapter to understand the significance of the modalities in a person's life.

With respect to sensory modalities in Benjamin Franklin's first memory, he describes the remembrance in a way that conveys a clear visual image. From purchasing the whistle, showing it off to his family, and then receiving bad news about the whistle's worth, visualizing the sequence of events emerges with ease for most people. As in his early recollection, the visual sense was conspicuous over the course of Franklin's life. His constant reading, work as a printer, scientist, inventor, writer, and extensive traveling all called upon his visual capacities. The sense of hearing is also notable in Franklin's first memory and is prominent in various aspects of his life. In his early recollection, family members verbally communicate to Ben the dubious value of the whistle after hearing him play it. Hearing was critical to Franklin in numerous endeavors, including his lifelong pursuit of music involving singing as well as writing songs, playing several musical instruments, and even inventing a new musical instrument, the armonica.[36] Franklin's auditory sense also enabled him to strategically listen to other people to acquire knowledge about the world and to empathically connect with individuals from all walks of life.

Beyond visual and auditory images, Franklin's early memory also includes the sense of touch. He exchanges money to purchase the whistle, and he holds the toy in his hand while bringing it to his lips. Franklin built his early reputation with his hands through his labor as a printer, therefore touch was a prominent modality in his life. His craft as a writer, use of musical instruments, tactile involvement with scientific experiments, and design of inventions all drew upon Franklin's touch sensitivities. In his early recollection, the senses of smell and taste are not a part of the narration. This does not mean that Franklin lacked a capacity or interest in the modalities; instead, they did not reach a level that fundamentally informed Franklin as to what life is like or about.

## Color

The visualization and experience of color vastly adds to the richness and beauty of life. Color enhances the vividness of objects and events and contributes to the security and well-being of humanity. Color often has an evocative effect on mood, and people value color in their natural and built locales. Relating to early recollections, on average one out of six people spontaneously report the presence of color in their remembrances.[37] Identifying particular objects, such as "the red chair" or "the green grass" and making general references to color, as in "the warm sun" or "the light was fading in the room," are common among those who cite color in their first memories. For these individuals, who may be considered "color-minded," color often assumes a key or even indispensable role in their everyday existence. A person may pay particular attention to color in the environment, and yearn for experiences with greater intensities of color. Ben Franklin, does not make reference to color in his first memory. As with most people this does not mean that he lacked an appreciation or sensitivity to color. Instead, his attunement to color is not at a level of intensity where it became an orientation to life. As a printer and inventor Franklin followed the craft of an artisan; he did not seem to possess the disposition or aesthetic sensitivities of an artist.

## Place

Partaking in events and experiences in life invariably occur in particular places or locations, and the quality of these environmental settings matter in terms of the well-being of individuals. Many people are able to describe or portray special places in which they prefer to spend time. For some individuals such a setting is indoors at home, and for others, a desirable locale is a natural environment near a river or a stream. Other persons do not necessarily have a strong preference for a particular location, and what goes on in the setting is what seems to matter most. In these instances, having people with whom to interact or the availability of certain activities or tasks is often more important than where the experiences happen. Relating to early recollections the location of the memory is usually ientifiable, including an individual's emotional reaction to the setting. Place is prominent and distinct in some first memories, and in other recollections the location seems secondary or incidental.[38] For a person with a memory in which the setting is evocative and conspicuous, the place may have either an uplifting appeal or evoke negative reactions. With positive emotions toward particular surroundings, an individual may experience a *sense of place* and gravitate to these settings in his or her life. The special environments are often found to have a captivating quality that is life-enhancing and stimulate a sense of emotional well-being. In contrast, an individual with adverse feelings toward a particular place in an early recollection may avoid or experience discomfort in a similar type of setting when encountered in life.

In Benjamin Franklin's early recollection, he journeys through the streets of Boston having a grand time blowing his new whistle until he arrives home. Franklin was physically mobile in his remembrance, and he appeared to find the most pleasure moving about his neighborhood. Franklin's connection to place does not seem to be limited to or defined by a particular location. In Franklin's life, he seemed to have few emotional ties to a place, and found visiting a variety of locations or settings gratifying.[39] Franklin frequently created desirable places by gathering around himself stimulating people and finding interesting ways to spend his time. Franklin was also fond of traveling, and his frequent trips took him on extended stays throughout the colonies and abroad. He lived in rented houses throughout his life, and never owned a home until his old age when he had a large brick house constructed in Philadelphia.[40]

## Objects

Most people are able to identify those favorite possessions which have a special meaning and importance. Family photographs, a hardwood table once owned by a grandparent, or an old pocket watch are examples of the countless number of items that individuals hold dear to them. In other instances material objects serve essential functions for sustaining and protecting life. Dwelling places in all of their expressions, various means of transportation, and technological devices that enhance productivity are representative of the vast range of objects that benefit humanity. With respect to early recollections, the recall of a memory almost always involves a reference to a particular object or objects.[41] In some remembrances, the physical presence of the entity is readily apparent, and the object may even be crucial to the meaning of a memory. As an example, consider the early recollection of a young girl playing with a doll and the centrality of the doll to the narration of the remembrance. In the memory, the doll is distinct in her pretty dress and shoes which evokes strong feelings of affection from the child. In many other first memories, objects are more of a background presence, only receiving a fleeting mention in the remembrance. For a person with notable objects that have an essential role in his early recollection, the objects potentially have a special meaning in the life of that individual. From the incalculable number of physical items that could possibly be remarked about in a first memory, certain objects seem to be recalled because they are evocative and are compatible with the interests and values of a person.

Two prominent and distinct objects, money and a whistle, arouse strong feelings from Benjamin Franklin in his early recollection. Franklin's gleeful exchange of his coppers for the whistle was a business transaction gone bad. However, both objects served as a means of access or a conduit for Franklin. The money enabled him to purchase a desirable toy, and the whistle brought attention to himself through a pleasurable experience. As in his first memory, particular objects were distinct in his life, but he engaged the entities in creative ways that went far beyond the largely self-serving focus of his remembrance. Franklin's trade as a printer in addition to his experiments in science and technology brought him into constant physical contact with objects. Typesetting, writing instruments, newspapers, and books were familiar to Franklin's hands for most of his life. Shrewd business dealings and the acquisition of money gave rise to many of Franklin's aspirations and accomplishments. His famous kite experiment, the lightning rod, bifocal glasses, the Franklin stove, and the armonica involved physical items that brought Franklin wealth and fame. All of the objects were close to Franklin's heart, but they also provided enduring contributions to the advancement of humanity.

In Franklin's early recollection, as a young child he endured a painful lesson of being taken advantage of due to his lack of wisdom of the ways of the world. The memorable transaction created a grounding for Franklin to pursue a quest for knowledge and experience which would serve to enlighten himself and others and bring him historical acclaim. Over the course of his life, Franklin showed a determination to maximize his potential by cultivating useful and stimulating outlets. In his life and writings, Franklin made it clear that striving to realize one's capacities and resources in harmony with humanity contributes to a more fulfilling existence.

# Chapter Six

# Capturing the "Big Picture"
## Core Themes and Early Recollections

From all of the millions of experiences to which we are exposed in our early childhood, we remember only those which coincide with our outlook on life.

—Rudolph Dreikurs[1]

In an early childhood memory a person privately constructs a convincing story that serves as an influential guide relating to what life is like or about. A core theme or central idea is almost always recognizable in the brief narrative of an individual's first memory that provides a unifying and compelling message. In Benjamin Franklin's early recollection, his personal story emphasizes the significance of a "lesson learned" as a thematic focus, as he came to the vexing realization that he had wasted his money on a foolish purchase. Although the dominant subject matter of an early recollection is unique to each person, particular themes in first memories tend to emerge with a relative degree of frequency.[2] For example, thematic content relating to demonstrating competency and enjoying the company of other people are somewhat common in early recollections. Thematic topics with less favorable conditions or outcomes also occur with some regularity in first memories and include such matters as neglect, victimization, and rejection. Furthermore, in most instances, when a person renders multiple early recollections, there are similarities among the themes of the remembrances. Based on the principle of the holistic unity of personality, the thematic focus of the memories usually supplements rather than contradicts one another.

## IDENTIFYING CORE THEMES
## IN EARLY RECOLLECTIONS

Capturing the central idea of an early recollection influences the meaning of the entire remembrance in key ways. A theme in a first memory relates to the events or what is occurring in the recollection. The emotions or feelings that a person has relating to the theme are also influential in understanding a memory's thematic content. In the interpretation process, for some early recollections, identifying a core theme is more directly apparent or explicit. Consider, for instance, the following first memory in terms of a prominent theme: "I remember printing my name on a piece of paper for the first time. I could see the letters of my name, and I felt so proud of myself." The thematic focus in this memory pertains to personal achievement and a sense of accomplishment. In other instances, recognizing a core theme is challenging and usually requires reflection in order to grasp the implied point of the early recollection. In Franklin's first memory, for example, his emotional reaction of "vexation" at the conclusion of the remembrance is crucial for understanding the meaning of its thematic message. Franklin's memory evokes a clear sense of loss but also a determination to do better and make amends, and this impression of Franklin gives rise to the theme of a lesson learned.

### Empathy and Thematic Analysis of Early Recollections

Attempting to maintain an empathic posture when listening to or reading accounts of early recollections facilitates a greater understanding of the remembrances. Essential components of empathy—including identification, imagination, and intuition—enable an individual to vicariously experience what it is like to be someone else for a fleeting period of time.[3] Although the early recollections of individuals vary widely in emotional intensity and specific circumstances, there is often sufficient commonality of human experience for a person attending to the remembrances to evoke a momentary sense of identification. The imaginative capacity of an individual also has a potential to stimulate emotions and images that are at least somewhat like those in another person's remembrance. A further human endowment that contributes to empathically understanding first memories is that of intuition. Intuitive reactions involve insights and hunches that immediately come to mind when processing accounts of early recollections. Finally, an individual may occasionally experience visceral sensations or physical reactions when reacting to the communication of evocative first memories. In the following early recollection example, the essential components of empathy enhance an understanding of the individual's remembrance, including its thematic focus.

## An Early Recollection of George

> I was about four or five years old and eating my oatmeal for breakfast at the kitchen table before going to school. All of the sudden, the bowl of oatmeal fell on my lap and onto the floor. My father started yelling at me and threw a rag on the floor for me to clean up the mess. I got down on my hands and knees to wipe up the oatmeal and the broken bowl, and my father kept hollering at me. Then he started wiping up the floor by pushing the rag around with his foot, I felt so stupid for what I did.

Making mistakes in life is a common and universal human experience. Identifying with George as he accidentally spills his oatmeal resonates without difficulty for most individuals. The visual portrayal of George, spilling the oatmeal and being on his hands and knees, readily emerges in one's imagination. Picturing George's father standing over him and shouting is a striking image. Experiencing an intuitive response or a "gut feeling" that George's father is excessively harsh, and that George takes the admonitions too much to heart is also a likely personal reaction. After all, George is a little boy and accidents happen. For some, George's remembrance may also evoke a slight tension in the stomach or chest when reading or listening to the account of the early recollection.

Empathy is essential when attempting to identify core themes of individuals in first memories. With respect to George's early recollection, an important focus of the remembrance involves an infliction of punishment. However, George's emotional reaction to his father's action is also essential to grasp the dominant theme of the memory. As a recipient of punishment, George reacts with guilt and a loss of self-respect. Even though most people would likely agree that George does not deserve the extent of his father's verbal abuse, this view is not reflective of George's immediate response. Empathically understanding the theme of George's early recollection means staying within his internal frame of reference or personal perspective as he absorbs the bcrating message. In this regard, as a core theme, George perceives that he had made a foolish and inexcusable blunder and is deserving of the chastisement.

## Follow-Up Questions in Early Recollections

Beyond the importance of employing empathy for understanding the meaning of an early recollection and identifying a core theme, particular follow-up questions are critical for clarifying a thematic focus.[4] In this regard, immediately after an individual recounts a first memory, ask: "Is there anything else that you can recall in the memory?" This question often elicits further information and details relating to the remembrance. The next question, however, is crucial for pinpointing the theme or the most vivid part of the remembrance: "What part do you remember most in the memory?" Another indispensable follow-up question to ask is: "How are you feeling at that point?" or "What feelings do you remember having then?" These questions frequently reveal the emotional reaction of a person to the thematic content of the remembrance. An interesting aspect to the last two follow-up questions is that individuals responding to these inquiries unknowingly identify the thematic message in their own remembrances.

## Early Recollections and Thematic Analysis

As identical triplets in their mid-twenties, Samantha, Jenna, and Krista shared their early recollections with me on separate occasions. Interestingly, although the sisters did not discuss their first memories with each other, there is a commonality in the core themes and emotional reactions of their remembrances. Further, the triplets even make use of similar terminology in their first memories, such as referring to the other sisters as "the girls."

### *Early Recollection of Samantha*

I was in the living room in my stroller and the girls were in their strollers. We were all bumping into each other. My grandparents were there. Jeopardy was playing on TV.

"*Is there anything else that you can recall in the memory?*" (Designated with "Details")

Details: "My grandparents visited every night."

"*What part do you remember most in the memory?*" (Designated with "Vivid")

Vivid: "Both my grandparents and the television."

"*How are you feeling at that point?*" or "*What feelings do you remember having then?*" (Designated with "Feelings")

Feelings: "I was probably happy and carefree."

The core theme of Samantha's early recollection emphasizes actively experiencing events in a lighthearted way.

## *Early Recollection of Jenna*

I feel that I can remember being maybe three years old sitting in a high chair or a stroller. There was music on. My parents were there and the girls of course.

Details: "My mother told me not to get into the twelve-pack of soda on the floor."

Vivid: "Getting into the soda."

Feelings: "Happy, energetic."

Similar to Samantha's remembrance, the core theme of Jenna's early recollection focuses on actively enjoying experiences in a carefree way—with a touch of mischievousness. Distinctive in Jenna's first memory is the auditory expressions involving music and the cautions of her mother.

## *Early Recollection of Krista*

Silly to remember. Being outside getting our picture taken with the girls and our great grandmother. We were two or three years old.

Details: "Our cousins were there too."

Vivid: "My great grandmother because she was old."

Feelings: "Happy, I guess."

As with her two other sisters, the theme of Krista's early recollection relates to enjoying a pleasant and rather carefree social experience. Unlike her sisters, Krista's remembrance takes place in an outdoor setting.

## SUBJECTIVE VIEWS AND CORE THEMES IN EARLY RECOLLECTIONS

A core theme in an early recollection generally conveys a person's evaluative sense of a memorable event or experience from a subjective perspective. Attempting to empathically understand the thematic content of a first memory from the vantage point of the individual recounting the remembrance is essential for an accurate interpretation. At the same time, an individual's thematic perspectives may be less than accurate in an objective sense or in terms of reality. As an example, Andrew's early recollection reveals that he maintains a core theme that people are indifferent to him and he is overlooked in life. In spite of environmental conditions in which a number of people extend him care and concern, Andrew continues to feel minimized and unimportant. In the case of Andrew and all people who communicate the central message of early recollections, what is most important to grasp is their subjective perspectives. These subjective ideas represent one's reality in the construction of a brief story of life.

*Chapter Seven*

# Becoming a Person

## *Personality Dimensions and Early Recollections*

I think, myself, that one's memories represent those moments which, insignificant as they may seem, nevertheless represent the inner self and oneself as most really oneself.

—Agatha Christie[1]

Attempting to describe the human personality can be challenging and usually involves identifying prominent and distinctive qualities of individuals. The use of everyday observations, such as "outgoing," "intense," and "serious," often captures aspects of a person's behavioral trends. Beyond such familiar expressions, various *personality dimensions* present a more formal or precise way to grasp the individuality of a person. Drawing from a lengthy list of psychological terms, particular characteristics emerge in the narrations of early recollections that contribute to defining patterns of behavior. In this regard, the dimensions of degree of activity, social interest, optimism and pessimism, self-efficacy, and conscientiousness represent a focus of broad research in the study of personality and in the literature on early recollections. These qualities are observable in the interactions of people and are possible to describe in behavioral terms. Although the dimensions represent enduring personality features, they are also subject to change and further development. An individual's awareness of unproductive or dysfunctional aspects of one's personality functioning and a determination to seek change foster a potential for growth in a constructive direction.

## THE MEANING OF PERSONALITY
## DIMENSIONS IN EARLY RECOLLECTIONS

When using the *Dawn of Memories* model, the interpretation of personality dimensions immediately follows an analysis of the core theme of an early recollection. The central idea or theme of a memory influences the meaning of personality trends, therefore an integration of thematic and personality domains is essential for accurately interpreting first memories. After introducing the psychological implications of each personality dimension and reference to thematic content, the relative strength of the qualities will be determined from diverse examples of individuals' recollections.

### Degree of Activity

*Psychological Implications*

In the view of Alfred Adler, an emotionally healthy degree of activity includes a pattern of initiative and engagement in the experiences of life coupled with an affinity with humanity through the expression of social interest.[2] An active orientation involves seeking out purposeful and constructive pursuits that are in harmony with other living beings. In a contrasting direction, Adler made reference to individuals with lower levels of activity and social interest who demonstrate maladaptive tendencies. Such people typically disengage from community-oriented endeavors and become passive or withdrawn. Generally, these individuals feel disinterested in or incapable of actively pursuing more participatory modes of existence. Adler also thought that a percentage of individuals exhibit high levels of activity, yet they do so with a deficient degree of social interest. In these instances, people actively pursue self-centered aims which may be damaging to others, with the most severe cases involving criminal and violent offenders. Adler thought that the degree of activity acquired in early childhood remains relatively stable over the life span unless individuals gain an insight into dysfunctional patterns and make a commitment to change.[3]

Researchers beyond Adler have given consideration to the active/passive quality of the human experience. Erika Fried, author of *Active/Passive: The Crucial Psychological Dimension*, thought that activity was vital to people as they exercise their skills and capacities in living.[4] Actively engaging in educational experiences, social contacts, recreational and health pursuits, in addition to numerous other productive facets of life, engenders vitality and positive emotions in a person. Patterns of purposeful activity and engagement in constructive tasks are also associated with longevity and life satisfaction.[5]

## Early Recollections

A relative degree of activity is often detectable in an individual's early recollections.[6] The consideration of various examples of first memories will contribute to clarifying the degree of activity in the following remembrances. Follow-up questions and a brief analysis will assist in understanding the core theme and the degree of activity of the person who relates each first memory.

### Early Recollection of Elaine

I remember going with my family to my grandmother's house that was a long way from where we lived. Nana had a big chest in a back room upstairs, and she let me and my younger sister look in it. Nana helped us put on some of the pretty clothes that were in the box, the dresses were really big.
"*Is there anything else that you can recall in the memory?*"
Details: "The dresses were mostly white."
"*What part do you remember most in the memory?*"

Vivid: "Opening the box and looking into it."

*"How are you feeling at that point?"* or *"What feelings do you remember having then?"*

Feelings: "Excited about finding what was in the box."

The theme of Elaine's first remembrance conveys a positive tone and suggests a curiosity and excitement for learning about new things. Elaine's degree of activity is high as she initiates actions and engages in a cooperative and engrossing task with her sister and grandmother.

## Early Recollection of Rosa

I was looking out the window of my house near the front door. A family was moving in across the street, and they had a big truck parked in front of their house. I thought about going over to see if there were any kids moving in, but I decided not to go over.

Details: "The truck was really big."

Vivid: "Looking at the truck and thinking about who was moving in."

Feelings: "Being afraid to go over."

The theme of Rosa's remembrance conveys a hesitant and apprehensive tone, and a sense of missing out on opportunities. Rosa's degree of activity is low, as she is uncertain about initiating actions.

## Social Interest

### Psychological Implications

Social interest is another personality dimension that Alfred Adler thought was a critical component of life in which a person strives to relate with other people in purposeful and constructive ways.[7] Social interest encompasses an individual's emotional identification with others that finds expression in cooperative and contributing endeavors. Empathy is an inherent aspect of social interest that involves an affinity with humanity and a desire to belong in a community.[8] Adler made reference to a *socially useful* type of person who combines a higher level of social interest with an elevated degree of activity.[9] Adler also identified individuals with low levels of social interest who typically feel alienated from other people and maintain a preoccupation with themselves.

An involvement with other people in constructive pursuits enables an individual to transcend oneself and gain a collective sense of support and personal affirmation. Making an active social contribution within a community enhances a person's meaning in life by becoming involved in endeavors with a larger purpose beyond one's own needs and preoccupations. In this regard, research suggests that individuals with broad social networks who engage in opportunities to reach out to or help others tend to live longer and experience more satisfaction and fulfillment in life.[10] Adler contended that social interest is acquired in early childhood and remains relatively stable over the life span of a person.[11] At the same time, Adler recognized that an insight into one's conception of life may promote the development of social interest when there is an accompanying commitment to change in a constructive direction.

## Early Recollection of Samantha

We were building a new house and my dad and some of his friends from work and my uncles were all there helping him to work on it. I was walking around with a play dress on which I was holding up in my hands to make a pocket out of it. I had nails in the pocket I had made and was carrying them around for my dad and uncles to use. I remember feeling like I was a really big help.

Details: "No, not really, I was probably around four years old."

Vivid: "Helping out my dad."

Feelings: "I remember feeling really happy because I felt like I was being such a good helper."

The contributory theme of Samantha's early recollection is compatible with the personality dimension of social interest. She is content in her helping role which conveys a high level of social interest.

### Early Recollection of Peter

> I think that I was in the second grade. I was waiting on the playground at recess to beat up a kid that I really hated because he was such a wimp. When he came out the door of the school, he saw me and starting running. I caught up to him and pushed him down in the snow. Then I punched him in the face. It felt good to see him cry like a baby.
> Details: "I hurt my foot running, but I was ok."
> Vivid: "Hitting him."
> Feeling: "It was exciting."

Aggression is thematic in Peter's early recollection as he delights in victimizing another person. Peter's hostile actions and lack of empathy and remorse indicate a low level of social interest.

## Optimism/Pessimism

### Psychological Implications

As a personality dimension, optimism relates to an individual's expectation of the likelihood of favorable events taking place and maintaining a positive outlook on life.[12] Pessimism involves an expectation that unfavorable events tend to occur and a negative outlook on life. With an anticipation of success, an optimistic person generally persists with tasks and adapts to challenging situations and adversities. Individuals with an optimistic outlook typically pursue active problem-solving strategies and bounce back relatively quickly from setbacks and hardships.[13] Optimistic people usually perceive fewer subjective reasons for anxiety or despair in comparison to pessimists, and, consequently, optimism is a predictor of satisfaction in life and longevity.[14] In a contrasting direction, a pessimistic individual frequently maintains low expectations for success and withdraws from or avoids challenging situations and adversities. With a passive coping approach in the face of stress, a person with a pessimistic outlook tends to make minimal efforts to adapt to or weather adverse conditions. In terms of emotional disorders, pessimistic trends are associated with depression and chronic arousal relating to anxiety.[15]

## Early Recollection of Patrick

I was about four years old playing in the back of our house in a garden with my mother and father. It was a nice warm day, late in the afternoon. My father was working in the garden with a shovel, and my mother was sitting on a blanket. I saw some buttercups growing on the edge of the field that were really pretty. I picked a buttercup and ran over to give it to my mother. She was so happy when I gave it to her.

Details: "The buttercups were bright yellow."

Vivid: "Running as fast as I could to give the buttercup to my mother."

Feelings: "Excitement and happiness."

Thematically, Patrick's early recollection portrays an expectation of a joyous event taking place as a result of his caring act. Patrick's awareness of his mother's happiness along with the idyllic tone of the remembrance suggests a high level of optimism on his part. Patrick also demonstrates an elevated degree of activity and strong social interest in his first remembrance.

## Early Recollection of Jeremy

I remember it was my birthday, and only a few kids came to my party. We started playing Pin the Tail on the Donkey, but I wasn't having any fun, so I quit playing. I got some presents, but they weren't what I wanted. One of the presents was a wooden top that was pretty stupid.

Details: "The cake had a clown on it."

Vivid: "Opening the presents and looking at them."

Feelings: "I felt let down and kind of tense."

Thematically, the early recollection portrays an event which should be enjoyable and special but is found to be disappointing.

The emotional tone of Jeremy's remembrance is bleak and dejected, suggesting a pessimistic outlook on life.

## Self-Efficacy

*Psychological Implications*

Self-efficacy relates to an expectation of success in managing demanding situations and overcoming obstacles. Persons with higher levels of self-efficacy generally believe that they are able to accomplish difficult tasks and successfully respond to challenges.[16] Albert Bandura, a psychology professor at Stanford University, originally formulated the term *self-efficacy* in 1977, and today there is a vast body of literature supporting the importance of self-efficacy in promoting healthy behaviors, academic achievement, career success, and numerous other human pursuits.[17] In these endeavors, persons with elevated levels of self-efficacy tend to set higher achievement goals and persevere in meeting challenges and effecting positive outcomes. Bandura observed that individuals who demonstrate higher self-efficacy have more control over their cognitions or thinking patterns and for the most part are capable of calming themselves in anxiety-provoking situations.[18] Persons with a reduced level of self-efficacy are less likely to feel capable of successfully coping with demanding situations. The association of low self-efficacy with stress, anxiety, and depression has been documented through numerous studies.[19] Bandura believed that there is a potential to change a person's ingrained belief in his or her diminished ability to do something of a challenging nature, and this pursuit has a greater and more enduring impact than merely reinforcing the individual to perform the task.[20]

*Early Recollection of Kindra*

I believe that I was around five years old, and was in the neighbor's backyard with my brothers and two neighborhood boys. We were all playing on the swing set. The boys challenged me to jump up and grab the rings that were wrapped high around the top bar. I did it. I grabbed one of the rings but I couldn't get the second one. I fell to the ground, and I landed on my wrist and it hurt. I ran back to my house telling my mom that I had fallen and hurt my wrist. The boys laughed when it happened, but they were concerned that I might be really hurt.

Details: "I remember being in the hospital but not being extremely scared or crying about it. I remember the cast and finally crying about the pain later in the evening."

Vivid: "Really wanting to jump, grab the rings and be successful. I wanted to meet the challenge."

Feelings: "Some anxiety I guess but also just feeling eager to meet the challenge."

The early recollection theme suggests a determination to succeed in a challenging situation. Kindra's belief in her ability to manage the situation and overcome obstacles indicates that she has a high level of self-efficacy.

## Early Recollection of Esther

We had chickens in the backyard, and one time I had to feed them. It was cold outside. I tried pushing on the door of the chicken coop, but it was too hard to get open. I didn't know what to do; so I threw the chicken feed behind a big tree and ran back into the house.

Details: "There was snow on the ground, and the chicken coop looked like an old shack."

Vivid: "Throwing the chicken feed behind the tree."

Feelings: "Scared that I'd get caught, but relieved that I could go back into the warm house."

Thematically, the memory relates to a failure to successfully negotiate and complete a challenging task. Esther's perception of her inability to cope and accompanying anxiety suggests a low level of self-efficacy.

## Conscientiousness

*Psychological Implications*

As a personality dimension, conscientiousness involves various components that include reliability, orderliness, perseverance, industriousness, and impulse control.[21] Typically, a person with an elevated level of conscientiousness is goal-directed and self-disciplined, enabling him or her to seek and accomplish goals.[22] In personality theory, conscientiousness is one of the "Big Five" traits that are classified as fundamental dimensions of human behavior.[23] In the research literature, conscientiousness is associated with well-being, better health, career success, and longevity.[24] Evidence also shows that the domain of conscientiousness tends to increase over the life span from young adulthood through late adulthood.[25] As individuals emotionally invest in family relationships and work, these commitments to social institutions frequently promote their level of conscientiousness. People with low levels of conscientiousness tend to be unreliable, disorganized, aimless, and impulsive.[26] Although conscientiousness represents an ingrained behavior trend, a person may slowly cultivate the trait with a determination to change and a sustained effort to build new behavioral patterns.

*Early Recollection of Vincent*

I was playing in the sand with my younger brother at the beach. We were making the castle. I was in charge and decided to build a few walls and moats around the middle of the castle. My little brother couldn't help much, so I gave him a small bucket to go get water for the moats. The sand kept breaking away once we put the water in the moats, so we built the walls even bigger.

Details: "I know my parents were with us, but they were not in the memory."

Vivid: "Seeing the water finally stay in the moats."

Feelings: "I felt good because it was kind of hard for us to do."

The theme of Vincent's early recollection suggests a determination to carry out a challenging task and get the job done right. The emotional tone of Vincent's remembrance conveys a sense of pride and a high level of conscientiousness for his efforts.

### *Early Recollection of Jacob*

I was in the second grade and had to stay in for recess because I got in trouble. Some old lady was watching me, and I told her that I had to go to the bathroom. On the way to the boys' room, I looked in a classroom. The room was empty so I went inside to look around. I picked up a few colored pencils off the desks and then went up to the teacher's desk. I thought that there might be some money around, but then I noticed a watch on the desk. I shoved it in my pocket and quickly left the room.

Details: "The watch was silver."
Vivid: "Seeing the watch."
Feelings: "Excited and wanting the watch."

The theme of the remembrance relates to victimizing other people. Jacob's lack of responsibility and impulse control suggests a low level of conscientiousness.

## EVALUATION AND DEVELOPMENT OF PERSONALITY DIMENSIONS

Evaluating personality dimensions and other aspects of an individual's way of being is possible through the use of early childhood recollections. When used as a personality assessment tool, early recollections provide glimpses into a person's characteristic strengths and other qualities that open pathways for growth and development. With an awareness of the qualitative level of personality functioning, an individual is in a more advantageous position to cultivate his capacities and potentialities. From another perspective, greater self-understanding enables a person to appreciate one's way of being in all of its uniqueness.

## Strengths in Personality Dimensions

The *Dawn of Memories* model focuses on five personality dimensions, with higher levels of the characteristics pointing to relative strengths in an individual's pattern of functioning or lifestyle. An insight into one's identifiable strengths enables a person to capitalize on the qualities when involved in various experiences in life. Each of the dimensions relates to effective and purposeful ways of engaging the world and emotional well-being. Particular characteristics suggest a relationship to longevity, life satisfaction, and meaning in life. Yet, as purposeful as the personality dimensions seem to be for positive mental health, there can be a downside to the qualities when they are rigidly maintained or engaged to excess. As an example, degree of activity hinders well-being if an individual frantically maintains a pursuit of activities to the point of depletion or exhaustion. A person may become so attuned to the concerns of others that her social interest disallows time to care for herself. A dose of reality is necessary for an individual with an overly optimistic outlook in order to deal effectively with unanticipated misfortunes in life. A person with high levels of self-efficacy must sensibly recognize conditions or situations that are beyond her capabilities or control. Acting responsibly is a key aspect of conscientiousness, but there are times when it is emotionally healthy to deliberately suspend a focus on responsibilities and fully enjoy an experience. As an example, taking a plunge into a cool lake on a hot day is not the time to worry about preparations for a family meal.

## Development of Personality Dimensions

Personality dimensions represent ingrained patterns of an individual's way of being. Without minimizing the challenge that enduring personality characteristics present for change, the qualities are subject to growth and development. With an awareness of unproductive or self-defeating personality dimensions and a determination to cultivate more purposeful functioning, an individual is in a more advantageous position to strategically pursue adaptive behavioral patterns. Making the effort to attempt small, deliberate, and persistent steps in the development of the personality characteristics is a sound way to enhance positive movement.[27] As an example, an elderly woman with a lowered degree of activity decides to take two walks a day and to plant a garden in her backyard. In another instance, in spite of a lessened expression of social interest, an adolescent makes a commitment to tutor a younger student on a weekly basis. A final example involves a young adult with a pessimistic outlook on life who acknowledges three positive situations that he experiences on a daily basis. Although progress is possible to effect incremental change in maladaptive personality trends through a personal commitment, deficits in an individual's psychological functioning as an individual may be of the magnitude that therapeutic intervention is necessary through the pursuit of personal counseling.[28]

*Chapter Eight*

# "I Am What I Perceive"

## *Perceptions and Early Recollections*

What we perceive and understand depends on what we are.

—Aldous Huxley[1]

Although the visual channel is the most dominant sense, the power of the other sensory endowments of hearing, touch, smell, and taste are also critical for engendering a flourishing human condition. Sense perceptions are detectable in early recollections and complement core themes and personality dimensions for understanding an individual's ingrained ways of being. People perceive the world in unique ways by means of their senses; therefore it is possible to identify sensory patterns in their first memories. The interpretation of early recollections further reveals personal affinities with perceptions of color, place or location, and material objects. Orientations to these perceptual modalities are frequently compelling and life-enhancing.

## SENSORY EXPRESSIONS
## AND EARLY RECOLLECTIONS

When individuals recount a first memory, they typically describe a visual image of being engaged in some type of activity in a particular setting. For most people, this pictorial portrayal takes place in silence, because sound rarely occurs in first memories. Representation of the other senses of touch, smell, and taste are also relatively rare. The comparative dominance of the visual modality has been supported in the research literature on early memories for more than one hundred years.[2] Yet, even though almost all individuals engage the visual channel in their first memories, a much smaller percentage of people also make reference to the other senses. The infrequent occurrence of sensory expressions beyond the visual modality raises questions about the significance of all the senses in early recollections and subsequently in life.

## The Sense of Vision and Early Recollections

### *Psychological Implications*

The capacity of sight enables human beings to partake in the richness and grand scope of existence through a visual endowment. Beyond aesthetic considerations, vision is crucial for the survival of the species and for successfully negotiating everyday life. The allure of visual stimulation is in keeping with the wide appeal of texting, instant messaging, video games, and other innovative technologies of the digital age. In early recollections, distinctive pictorial images depict innumerable situations and events in the human experience. Although visual imagery prevails in first memories in comparison to the other senses, there are variations in the intensity of the expressions. For many persons, first memories reflect a prominent and distinct sight-modality focus, and with others their remembrances assume a secondary or incidental visual emphasis.

Clear pictorial images in early recollections suggest that the faculty of vision may have an orienting influence in the life of a person. This high level of appeal possibly finds expression in such visual pursuits as reading, television and movies, observing people and events, and much more. Individuals with a visual orientation often "think" in pictures and readily engage in imaginary activities. Mentally visualizing experiences and situations is a significant aspect of the learning process for those who may be considered *visually minded*.[3] In a less favorable direction, the possibility exists that people with strong pictorial tendencies are drawn to visual activities to the point of minimizing or even avoiding their engagement of the other senses. As an example, visually minded individuals may find themselves using virtual world activities to excess, therefore potentially restricting their access to other vitalizing and broadening sense expressions.

## An Early Recollection of Bart

> I must have been around five years old, and my father took me to a baseball game at Fenway Park. I remember walking up the steps and seeing this amazing place in front of me. The field was a rich green color and everything sparkled. The players must have been warming up for the game because there were so many balls being hit and thrown all over the park. There were a lot of people in the stands, and our seats way were up high.
> Details: "I remember seeing the huge set of lights above the field."
> Vivid: "Walking up the stairs and looking all around the park."
> Feelings: "It was thrilling."

Thematically, Bart's early recollection relates to the delight of participating in an engrossing sensory experience. Bart actively engages his sense of vision, and the presence of color intensifies the visual impact of his memory.

## An Early Recollection of Nathan

> One day I had to walk home from school, and it was cold outside. My mother always picked me up in her car, but on this particular day I had to walk, and I'm not sure why. I remember being angry at my mother for not giving me a ride. It was pretty far to get home, maybe a mile or so.
> Details: "My mother should have told me that she was not going to pick me up."

Vivid: "Walking home and feeling angry."
Feelings: "Like I said, I was mad."

The theme of Nathan's first memory relates to a perceived breach of entitlement. From a sensory perspective Nathan's remembrance does not emphasize visual imagery.

## The Sense of Hearing and Early Recollections

*Psychological Implications*

Hearing is crucial to the functioning and sustenance of humanity in the vast realms of existence. The sense of hearing enables individuals to communicate with one another and to develop capacities for speech and language. With continual interactions in the environment, exposure to sound elicits stimulating, comforting, distressing and a broad range of other acoustic experiences that are fundamental to the quality of life. With respect to early recollections, sound is relatively rare and occurs in less than one out of twenty remembrances.[4] People with auditory images in their first memories often gravitate to sound and seek out aural stimuli. Consequently, hearing tends to have an orienting influence for these individuals and is a primary means for negotiating with and appreciating experiences in life. For these *hearing-minded* persons there is a captivating aspect to listening that finds expression in a wide variety of activities and contexts.[5] An individual with an orientation to hearing is drawn to such aural experiences as listening to music, a crackling fire, wind chimes, rain falling on a tin roof, and much more. These diverse stimuli frequently provide a means of relaxation or can be equally energizing. Typically, the hearing-minded person enjoys participating in conversations and likes to talk. In educational experiences, a hearing-oriented individual often finds that listening enhances the learning process, particularly with an emphasis on verbal interactions and face-to-face discussions. A person with an aural orientation also has a tendency to verbalize or talk out loud to oneself in the course of solitary activities.

## Early Recollection of Anna

> I grew up on a farm. Sometimes, before going to school it was my job to milk the cows. I must have been about six or seven years old, and I was walking to the barn. I could hear the cows mooing. It just seemed so pleasant because I felt that the cows needed me. It was really cold out, but I knew that the barn would be warmer when I got there.
>
> Details: "I could also hear the bells on a few of the cows ringing."
>
> Vivid: "Walking toward the barn and hearing the cows and the bells."
>
> Feelings: "A soothing feeling of contentment."

Thematically, Anna's early recollection emphasizes the anticipation of accomplishing a helpful task. With a clear auditory focus, Anna's remembrance elicits a blissful association.

## The Sense of Touch and Early Recollections

### Psychological Implications

From the moment of birth, touch is the most basic of the human senses as is demonstrated by the comfort an infant experiences with the caress of a loving parent. A baby receives intimate care through tactile stimulation when a parent or caregiver and an infant are in sustained contact with each other. Importantly, touch promotes psychological security and an environmental stability.[6] Without this contact infants often have difficulty forming secure attachments with people. As a human need throughout life, the touch of another person has a potential to communicate caring and understanding in addition to providing stress-reducing benefits. At the same time, another individual's touch may be gratuitous or even invasive, and in these instances touch is likely to have an adverse quality. For almost all people, sensual experiences, such as gently stroking a baby's smooth skin, putting on a warm sweater on a cold day, or sipping a beverage from a favorite cup lends a richness to life and enhances well-being.

Relating to early recollections, the engagement of tactile sensations is infrequent, occurring in less than ten percent of memories.[7] Individuals who receive or express physical touch in their remembrances tend to have an orientation to touch in their life and may be considered *touch-minded*.[8] A person with an affinity to touch typically seeks out tactile stimuli, such as a desire to receive affectionate touch, an urge to touch objects, as well as a preference for smooth textures in clothing. Those that are touch-minded tend to enjoy receiving and giving hugs, holding or gripping items in one's hands, receiving massages and back rubs, and are involved in a world of similar touch experiences. These individuals also may have a desire to cut tags off from shirts and pants that are irritating, wear soft slippers and other comfortable garments, enjoy a hot tub when good fortune makes it available, and prefer a silky fabric for their bedsheets. In touch activities as a child, he or she liked to climb trees, jump in piles of leaves, or roll down snow banks. From an educational perspective, hands-on pursuits that allow for an opportunity to manipulate materials and objects frequently enhances the learning process for individuals with an orientation to touch.

### Early Recollection of Sandra

My mother had a beautiful dressing table in her bedroom, and I remember on a winter evening sitting in front of the table while she was brushing my hair. My hair was kind of long and my mother brushed it gently with her large silver hairbrush. Her hands were soft when she touched my hair and head. It was kind of cold in the bedroom, and my mother wrapped me up in a snuggly blanket to keep me warm.

Details: "I think that I had just taken a bath."

Vivid: "My mother brushing my hair."

Feelings: "Pleasant and peaceful."

Thematically, Sandra's early recollection depicts a tranquil interpersonal experience. The emphasis on the sense of touch in Sandra's remembrance makes it especially poignant.

## The Sense of Smell and Early Recollections

*Psychological Implications*

In comparison to vision, hearing, and touch, the sense of smell seems less prominent and significant in everyday life. At the same time, odor perceptions are critical to survival by warning against toxic and harmful substances, and pleasant smells enrich human life through a vast array of stimulating and invigorating fragrances. Most people enjoy the appealing smells of a variety of evocative stimuli, while other unpleasant odors are often found to be repugnant. Fleeting scents have a capacity to trigger powerful images and evoke haunting memories from a long ago time.[9] When an adult sniffs an oiled baseball glove or experiences a whiff of hot homemade apple pie, he may be immediately transported to a memory as a child standing on a baseball field or helping his mother cook in the kitchen of his childhood home. Making reference to emotionally unforgettable memories, Rudyard Kipling writes, "Smells are surer than sounds or sights to make your heart strings crack."[10]

With respect to early recollections, reference to smells is rare, perhaps two or three remembrances out of one hundred.[11] The relatively few individuals who mention odor sensations in their first memories tend to have an orientation to smell in daily life. Such a *smell-minded* person appreciates a range of odor-related stimuli and seeks out fragrances that are often found to be mood-elevating and life-enhancing.[12] An individual with an orientation to smell generally enjoys a variety of synthetic or natural aromas that have an invigorating and uplifting effect. In indoor settings, pleasant odors from foods, candles, aromatic devices, essential oils, body lotions and sprays, fresh flowers, and perfumes may be particularly appealing. In natural environments, access to fresh air, fresh cut grass, flowers and herbs in a garden, and burning wood are among a number of scents that are alluring to many smell-minded persons. At the same time, these individuals usually find stale or foul odors aversive and typically avoid experiencing smells that are repugnant or nauseating.

## An Early Recollection of Janet

We used to live in a big white house and way back in the yard there was a lot of lilac bushes. I was about five years old and remember sitting under the lilacs on a bench playing with my doll. I could smell the lilacs that were all around me. It was a beautiful day, and the smell from the lilacs was delightful. I held my doll up to the lilac bushes and let her smell them.

Details: "My mother was nearby doing something in the yard."

Vivid: "Bending my head back and holding a lilac bush so that I could smell it better."

Feelings: "It was intense, almost intoxicating."

The theme of Janet's early recollection suggests an awareness and appreciation of a sensory condition of nature. Janet's sense of smell is prominent and compelling in her remembrance.

## The Sense of Taste and Early Recollections

### Psychological Implications

From infancy through old age, individuals engage in countless sensations of taste through the consumption of food and liquids. A satisfying meal, a tasty snack, or a favorite hot or cold drink are among the pleasures of life that people enjoy on a daily basis when they are fortunate enough to have access to such gustatory experiences. The sense of smell contributes to the quality and the perception of taste, and varying cultural experiences are influential in affecting individuals' food preferences across the world. Although the experiences of taste are constant throughout life on a daily basis, the modality is rarely present in a first memory. Theoretically, as a biological drive, taste may be so compelling that it does not require the motivational impetus inherent in early recollections for capturing what life is like or about. Yet, although taste seldomly materializes in first memories, for some people the modality is prominent and distinct, therefore taste possibly serves an orienting influence in their life.

With respect to early recollections, reference to taste expression is sparse, occurring in perhaps one or two out of one hundred remembrances with individuals who may be considered the *taste-minded*.[13] This affinity to taste generally results in a desire to explore and consume a variety of foods and drinks. The taste-oriented person, when old enough to do so, often seeks out new foods and restaurants as well as learning about culinary experiences. Spending considerable time selecting foods and drinks for meals and events and generating new recipes and cuisines are typical pursuits. Ironically, an orientation to taste does not necessarily mean that the person enjoys cooking. However, some individuals with an affinity to taste relish cooking and may even find a career or a vocation in the culinary arts appealing.

### An Early Recollection of Peter

I remember visiting my aunt's old house in the country with my mother, father, and younger sister. My parents were talking with my aunt in the kitchen, and my sister and I were playing around the dining room table. On the top of the table my aunt had some red apples in a big bowl with some other fruit. I wanted an apple, so I took a bite out of one. It tasted delicious, so I took another bite out of a few more of the apples. Each new apple seemed sweeter than the one that I had just tasted. I turned the apples around so you couldn't see where I had bitten into them.

Details: "Most of the apples were bright red and really juicy."
Vivid: "Biting into the apples and enjoying how sweet they tasted."
Feelings: "I felt happy."

The theme of Peter's early recollection has an active and playful quality with a focus on a gustatory experience. Peter's sense of taste is notable and distinct in his remembrance.

## Sensory Variations and Early Recollections

For many individuals, visual scenes constitute the only sense representation in their early recollections. In the first memories of other persons, two or more prominent sensory expressions emerge in their remembrance. When multiple senses are compelling in early recollections, each sense may have an orienting influence. While this dynamic combination is potentially enriching for a person, at times the sensory effect may also be distracting or overstimulating. In a far rarer occurrence, a very small percentage of individuals describe an overlapping or blending of sense expressions in an early memory and in life. Known as *synesthesia*, one sensory process stimulates another and there is an interweaving of the senses. As an example, tasting something triggers a person's sense of hearing in a form of cross-wiring. Another sense variation includes people who experience sensory impairments. An interesting question that arises from this condition: how do individuals with limitations in their sense modalities, such as in vision or hearing, formulate and describe their early recollections?

## Multiple Senses and Early Recollections

*Psychological Implications*

A number of people make reference to multiple sense perceptions in the recounting of their early recollections. The activation of the prominent senses that emerge in a person's first memories is often stimulating and invigorating in life. An orientation to particular senses frequently enhances the richness and complexity of life experiences and events. For example, as an adult, Diana has visual, auditory, and smell sensitivities that are distinctive in her early recollections and in her everyday existence. On a Sunday afternoon while sitting on a park bench, Diana simultaneously views people walking by, hears the sounds of birds chirping, and smells roasted peanuts cooking. Diana, and others like her with multiple orientations to particular senses, maintain an attunement to sensory perceptions that elicits personal attention and is often captivating. Such individuals may also notice details or impressions involving the senses that are often overlooked by other people. In a less favorable direction, a person with an orientation to multiple senses may at times find the activation of sense expressions to be distracting or inducing a sensory overload. Various environmental stimuli possibly trigger multiple senses, and focusing on a particular task involving a single sense, such as listening, may be momentarily challenging. In other instances, engaging multiple senses over prolonged periods of time has a potential to be mentally fatiguing or physically draining. For these individuals, finding a respite from excessive sense activation through such pursuits as meditation or listening to background music can be helpful and adaptive.

## An Early Recollection of Frank

I remember visiting my cousin Ernie and his family on a summer vacation, and they had an electric train set in the basement of their house. The train went around a track that was set up with little houses and stores. I shifted a gauge on the transformer to make the train go faster or slower. There was a burning smell that came from the transformer, and we put powder in the smoke stack of the big black locomotive to make it puff smoke. The locomotive also had a loud whistle that we used a lot. A couple of times the train went off the track because it was going so fast.

Details: "The train also rode by a farm and a forest area."

Vivid: "When the train flew off the tracks sparks went flying, and there was a crashing sound."

Feelings: "It was captivating and a lot of fun."

Thematically, the early recollection portrays an absorbing and entertaining multisensory experience. In the remembrance, with the exception of taste, Frank engages all of his senses.

## Synesthesia and Early Recollections

### Psychological Implications

Synesthesia involves the stimulation of one sense involuntarily triggering another sense modality. Instead of remaining separate, there is a blending of two or more senses in a type of cross-pollination. Synesthetes (people who experience synesthesia) have a capacity to hear sound as a color, see letters or shapes in color, or even hear taste.[14] Synesthesia runs in families and is a statistically rare condition, with percentages ranging from 1 in 200 persons to more intense cases numbering about 1 in 5,000 people.[15] One theory attributes the causation of synesthesia to a physical cross-wiring of neural connections in the brain that are normally separate.[16] In a case example, Melissa Lee, a college professor of English, is a synesthete who finds that synesthesia particularly affects how she remembers information. Melissa recalls names, lines from literature, telephone numbers, certain French and Spanish vocabulary words, and various other types of information through color associations. For example, according to Melissa, she perceives the days of the week in French as fuchsia, blue, yellow, deep red, plain red, yellow with black spots, and a slightly lighter fuchsia. Melissa states that synesthesia enriches her life and has been beneficial for learning. Some other synesthetes find the condition to be distracting in certain circumstances. At the same time, most synesthetes have a positive view of synesthesia and value its stimulating quality. In her early recollection, Melissa experiences a variety of colors in each of the numbers that come to mind as she repeats them to her mother.

## An Early Recollection of Melissa

My dad went on business trips a lot, and I got to sleep with my mom. The morning of my fourth birthday, I was lying down with my face in the pillow. I said "No more three, only four." As I said it, the three in my mind was red and the four was blue. The pillows were cream-colored, and my mom was wearing the red house coat that she always wore. I remember hearing my mom moving around me in the room and I can hear the swish of the red coat.

Details: "Pretty much what I explained."

Vivid: "The colors of the numbers as I said the words in my head."

Feelings: "Very happy that it was my birthday and the numbers were pretty. I like seeing colors."

Thematically, Melissa's early recollection emphasizes her delight in discovering a new and stimulating experience. As a synesthete, she visualizes letters and numbers in color in her remembrance.

## Sensory Impairments and Early Recollections

*Psychological Implications*

For a small percentage of individuals, intriguing questions arise about the relationship of their sensory impairments to the processing and communication of their early recollections. Although investigations on the topic are minimal, one study by Robert Lee Williams, a professor at Gallaudet University, and John Bonvillian, a professor at the University of Virginia, gave consideration to the first memories of hearing impaired college students. In an unanticipated research finding, deaf persons evaluated their initial recollections significantly more positively than hearing individuals.[17] Williams and Bonvillian were somewhat surprised by this data due to their assumption that deaf persons would likely experience more frustration and loneliness in their early childhood in comparison to the hearing endowed, and this would be reflected in the content of their first memories. In an even more unexpected result, deaf individuals reported that their initial first remembrances occurred around three-and-a-half years of age. This finding was surprising because deaf children of hearing parents typically do not acquire adequate sign language skills until after several years of formal education. In other words, the deaf persons were able to formulate their early recollections before acquiring more developed speech skills. This outcome raises doubt about the belief that a sufficient degree of competency in language is necessary to generate and retain first memories.

Another sensory line of inquiry relates to the experiencing of early recollections of the visually impaired. Considering that processing a first memory seems to universally elicit a visual image, how does a blind person formulate an early childhood memory?

Most often people picture themselves engaging in some type of activity in their early recollections; yet, creating a visual memory is beyond the capacity of most blind individuals. In particular, the congenitally blind are born without sight and have never experienced concrete visual images.[18] Importantly, blind persons often rely on their sense of touch for providing spatial information and sensorial clues about the world.[19] To evaluate how blind individuals experience their early recollections, Roger Beaudoin, a social worker in private practice, volunteered to recount his first memories. Roger is congenitally blind.

### Early Recollections of Roger

When I was four years old, I had one of those cars that you sit on, and I was peddling along, and I did not know where I was going. A neighbor saw me and guided me over to a gas station. I asked him why I was going there, and he said he needed to fix my tires. He called my parents, and they came and me picked up.

Details: "I got a pretty good spanking for being in the road."

Vivid: "Peddling."

Feelings: "Having a good time enjoying myself. The neighbor was a pretty friendly guy, and I was pretty trusting at the time."

Thematically, Roger's early recollection conveys the enjoyment of a physical and exploratory activity. In the absence of visual images, Roger engages auditory and touch sensations in his remembrance. In his next early memory, Roger experiences additional sensory modalities.

I was five and living in Colorado Springs at the time. I was in kindergarten in Mrs. Greaton's class. We were playing with clay; I was a big clay fan. I tried eating it but it didn't taste good. She said, "Roger, that was clay." I did like that part—getting attention.

Details: "Gritty clay, cold, yet soft. I could shape it, and it had a certain smell."

Vivid: "Trying to eat the clay. I could feel the texture on my tongue."

Feelings: "I felt pretty good about it. It was fun."

The theme of Roger's early recollection has an experiential and exploratory focus. With the exception of vision, Roger's remembrance includes all of the senses—hearing, touch, smell, and taste. Interestingly, although Roger did not visualize his first memories, in reading the remembrances sighted persons readily bring to mind visual images of a little boy peddling a small car and attempting to eat clay.

## PERCEPTIONS OF COLOR, PLACE, AND OBJECTS IN EARLY RECOLLECTIONS

Beyond the sense modalities in early recollections, other human perceptions provide insights into the realm of personality functioning. Colors, places or locales, and objects are abundant in the environment, and some individuals have an affinity with the precepts that is life-orienting and integral to their way of being. The experience of color in a person's first memories suggests a heightened sensitivity to the wonder of color in everyday life. When the physical location or material objects are notable in early recollections, the perceptions may be particularly influential in the life of the person.

### Color and Early Recollections

*Psychological Implications*

The visual experience endows the human spirit with the richness and aesthetic beauty of the perception of color. An enhancement of the vividness of events and objects occurs through an infusion of the color spectrum. Access to the captivating world of color is available to most people, and an appreciation and interest in color is universally recognizable across cultures. Relating to early recollections, reference to color occurs in a minority of first memories, with about one in six persons spontaneously observing color.[20] Individuals who cite color in their early recollections appear to have a heightened appreciation and sensitivity toward color that is more intense and compelling in comparison to what most people experience. This aesthetic disposition does not mean that the person has an exceptional artistic talent; instead, it is more about how the individual perceives and values color. Those with first memory representations of color may be considered to be *color-minded*, as they seek out and have a longing for a variety of colors in their environment.[21] Such people find color stimulating and enriching and frequently experience a desire to locate color in their lives. This orientation possibly finds expression in personal attire, home decorations, and observing color configurations in both the built and natural worlds. To the color-minded, colors often have a mood-enhancing effect, and random appearances of hues can be invigorating and even inspirational. At the same time, an absence or a clashing of colors can be distressing to their aesthetic sensibilities.

### An Early Recollection of David

I must have been around five years old and I was visiting my grandmother with my parents and sister. I remember walking through the rooms in her house and seeing all of the vibrant colors in each room that caught my eye. I could see the decorations, rugs, and pictures. Some of the wooden floors were covered by what I know now as Oriental rugs. The reds and blues in the rugs were rich and beautiful.

Details: "In one room the big windows had light colored yellow curtains, and I liked this room the best."

Vivid: "There were so many rich colors and objects that I was caught up in it all."

Feelings: "Captivated."

The theme of David's early recollection emphasizes his participation in an engrossing aesthetic experience. David finds color to be arresting in his remembrance.

## Place and Early Recollections

*Psychological Implications*

People often have an emotional relationship with a place or location that holds a special meaning in their lives. The setting may be a childhood home, a lake that has been a spot for family gatherings, a backyard garden, or some other locale with a special appeal. In other instances, for individuals who have had adverse or unpleasant experiences in a setting, these environments may trigger negative associations and reactions. Relating to early recollections identifying the settings in the remembrances is usually possible. In some first memories, the place is conspicuous and distinct, and in other recollections the location assumes a secondary or incidental quality.[22] When a place is notable in an early recollection, an individual may have a favorable or unfavorable emotional reaction toward that locale. With positive feelings toward a place, a person frequently gravitates to the setting and finds it to be restorative or enriching. Finding oneself in certain places, such as the built environment of the home or the natural surroundings of a wooded area, gives rise to a sense of well-being. Spending time in these settings is often uplifting and life-enhancing. In this sense, the individual may be considered to be *place-minded* due to a strong valuation and attention to locales that have an intangible quality.[23] This orientation often includes a sensitivity to a *sense of place* that imbues special settings with a beloved allure and appreciation that resonates within the person.[24]

In a contrasting direction, individuals may experience negative feelings toward a place that is recognizable in their early recollections. This adverse reaction has a potential to surface in similar types of settings at subsequent points in a person's life. As an example, as a middle-aged adult, Todd recounts two early memories in which he was subjected to humiliation and ridicule on a school bus. Many years after the episodes, Todd experiences an underlying tension and unease whenever he must board a bus.

## An Early Recollection of Melissa

I remember driving in the car with my parents, looking out the window. Seeing a farm and thinking: "That's what I want to have someday." It was so pretty.

Details: "I was in this big green station wagon. The house was white and red, and everything was green."

Vivid: "I can picture what the farm looked like—a barn and the landscape all around it."

Feelings: "Excited; realizing that I want to have that. It seemed like it was far away but that I could have it."

Thematically, Melissa's early recollection has an anticipatory quality as she delights in seeing the farm. There is a longing for the special place that is grounded in its immediate allure.

## Objects and Early Recollections

### Psychological Implications

Material objects have always had a significant influence in support of the survival and evolving condition of humanity. Objects represent a vast range of tangible items and devices, such as tools for earning a living, personal possessions, and various means of transportation. Similar to place in early recollections, objects are either prominent or distinct in the remembrance or they assume a secondary or incidental role.[25] A toy, piece of furniture, compass, bicycle, or other items from the world of objects may be the focus of attention in an individual's first memory. When objects elicit a positive response in one's remembrance, the person may have an affinity with articles that is orienting in life. In this regard, various items often engender a sense of satisfaction and well-being, prompting the individual to be *object-minded*.[26] As an example, Rory, in his early recollection, finds delight in playing with a construction set as he builds a set of toy houses and buildings from a variety of wooden blocks. As an adult, Rory has always enjoyed working with his hands and constructing projects. The object in an early recollection may also serve as a vehicle that contributes to the desired outcomes in the memory and in life. Consider, for instance, in a variation of Rory's remembrance another individual joins him in the construction tasks, and Rory prefers this mutual involvement. Consequently, in his everyday life, Rory finds the most satisfaction in building pursuits that include the companionship of other people.

When particular objects, such as coins, dolls, or tools, evoke a positive emotional reaction in an early recollection an individual may have a desire to acquire or spend time with these items in life contexts. On the other hand, objects that evoke adverse or negative reactions in first memories may be subsequently avoided. From another perspective relating to objects in early childhood, children frequently hold dear a special object, such as a cuddly doll, a warm blanket, or a soft cloth. This cherished item generally helps in managing the distress of a parent's periodic absence and is considered a *transitional object*.[27] The possession is indispensable to the child who often carries it around and falls asleep holding the object. After much use, the item usually gets soiled or worn out, but the child refuses to relinquish it. In time, the young child tends to spend less time with the object and eventually puts it away or loses track of the item. Interestingly, given the significant time and devotion that children expend with transitional objects, the items are rarely mentioned in early recollections. This omission possibly occurs because the object is not integral to an individual's lifestyle or perception of what life is like or about.

## An Early Recollection of Henry

I remember my father showing me an old pocket watch when I was quite little. The watch was gold and inscribed with a locomotive train on the front. My father opened the front cover of the watch, and the black numbers were sparkling in contrast to the white background. He then shut the front cover and opened the back lid of the watch. There were all kinds of gears and springs in there.

Details: "The watch was on a gold chain and he put it in my shirt pocket."

Vivid: "Seeing the gears spinning around."

Feelings: "I was amazed."

Thematically, the early recollection conveys Henry's excitement when interacting with the captivating object. Henry's reference to color intensifies the visual image of the object.

## INDIVIDUAL DIFFERENCES IN PERCEPTIONS AND EARLY RECOLLECTIONS

People who have an orientation to the senses, color, place, or objects contribute to humanity in a way that is influential beyond self-interest and personal gratification. With an affinity to these precepts, the individuals often provide powerful reminders for all of us about how the splendid facilities enrich the human condition. It is easy to take sight, hearing, physical objects and places, and other perceptions for granted and become complacent about their existence. Whether it is the color-minded individual who marvels at the spectrum of colors or the person with an orientation to smell finding joy in the natural fragrances of nature, witnessing such emotional reactions often stimulates other people with a fresh awareness and appreciation for the wonders of the perceptual world. From another perspective, at times an individual may be critical toward oneself or endure criticism from others for excessively engaging in activities involving perceptions that are orienting in life. When a person experiences certain perceptions, such as the allure of color or a frequent desire to touch, an insight into the deep and enduring nature of these compelling functions can be liberating. The uniqueness of a person involves an ingrained affinity toward particular perceptual modalities that is inherent to one's way of being. Additionally, with an increase in sensitivity toward people with orienting perceptions, there is an accompanying enhancement of empathic understanding that is beneficial in human relationships.

*Part III*

# TRADITIONS AND PRACTICES OF EARLY RECOLLECTIONS

*Chapter Nine*

# Teaching by Example
## *Early Recollections of Historical Figures*

The longer you can look back, the further you can look forward.

—Winston Churchill[1]

Illuminating resources exist in the published chronicles of historical figures who have disclosed early childhood memories in various accounts of their lives. Leonardo da Vinci, Dwight David Eisenhower, Martin Luther King Jr., along with other illustrious individuals have made reference to their early recollections, and in doing so have allowed the public to gain a deeper understanding of their life stories.[2] Of course, when assessing published first memories, valuable face-to-face exchanges and follow-up questions are not possible to implement. However, access to the vast breadth of materials about the luminaries provides rich sources of information that are typically not available when eliciting early recollections on an interpersonal basis. Through the *Dawn of Memories* model, the first remembrances of three historical figures will be evaluated in the narrative contexts of their lives.

As world-renowned personalities, Thomas Jefferson, Albert Einstein, and Mother Teresa disclosed early childhood memories that achieved posterity in published documents. Thomas Jefferson, twice elected president of the United States, is the author of the Declaration of Independence. Albert Einstein worked his way from an obscure government position to become an eminent scientist and an iconic global figure. Mother Teresa, as a nun serving the poorest of the poor, became one of the most famous women in the world. Although there are commonalities in the characteristics of these celebrated individuals, such as a high degree of activity, there are also clear distinctions in their ways of being and in the diversity of their life stories. In several instances, the historical figures exhibit exceptional personal qualities that are notable in their first memories. For example, Thomas Jefferson's early recollections depict a strong affinity with place that was also prominent in his life.

## THE LIFE AND EARLY
## RECOLLECTIONS OF THOMAS JEFFERSON

Thomas Jefferson was born in the spring of 1743 on a frontier farm at Shadwell in Virginia. When he was two years old, Jefferson moved with his family to a large plantation in Tuckahoe, fifty miles away.[3] After seven years, the family returned to Shadwell, the land where Jefferson would later build his beloved home, which he would name "Monticello." In his youth, Jefferson had access to a vast countryside for exploring, and he simultaneously benefited from a classical education. With a brilliant and capacious mind, Jefferson's scholarly and practical pursuits were wide-ranging: agriculture, archeology, science, architecture, gardening, farming, inventions, astronomy, philosophy, and botany. Later in his career in government, as governor of Virginia he narrowly escaped being apprehended by British soldiers when they occupied Monticello in 1781.[4] As a member of the Continental Congress in 1776, Jefferson called upon his superb language skills and creative energies in drafting the Declaration of Independence. Subsequently, while serving as a minister to France, Jefferson was asked to become the first Secretary of State of the United States by George Washington.

In 1796 Jefferson became vice president, and in 1801 ascended to the office of president of the United States. As president, Jefferson authorized the Louisiana Purchase from France, more than doubling the size of the nation in a westward expansion. In another major accomplishment, he cut the national debt by one-third.[5] After completing his second term as president, Jefferson retired to Monticello where he resided for seventeen years until his death on the Fourth of July, 1826. In retirement at Monticello, Jefferson enjoyed the company of his daughter Martha and his grandchildren. Only two of Jefferson's six children lived into adulthood, with only Martha surviving him. Jefferson was fond of his daily two-hour horseback rides at Monticello, and also pursued a variety of other activities including reading, farming, letter writing, and overseeing further construction on his property. In his culminating effort to advance humanity, Jefferson assumed key administrative and architectural roles in the creation and design of the University of Virginia.

Two of Thomas Jefferson's first memories appeared in *The Domestic Life of Thomas Jefferson: Compiled from Family Letters and Reminiscences*, written by Jefferson's great-granddaughter, Sarah Randolph in 1871.[6] As a direct descendent of Thomas Jefferson, Randolph captured essential elements of Jefferson's remembrance.

> Thomas Jefferson was not more than two years old when his father moved to Tuckahoe, yet he often declared that his earliest recollection in life was of being, on that occasion, handed up to a servant on horseback, by whom he was carried on a pillow for a long distance.[7]

> He also remembered that later, when he five years old, he one day became impatient for his school to be out, and, going out knelt down behind the house, and there repeated the Lord's Prayer, hoping thereby to hurry up the desired hour.[8]

## AN INTERPRETATION OF THOMAS JEFFERSON'S EARLY RECOLLECTIONS

### Core Themes

In Thomas Jefferson's first memory, which I refer to as the *pillow recollection*, there is an immediate promise of a pleasant passage

through the woodlands as he is lifted up into the open arms of a ser-
vant to be placed on a pillow. The sublime quality of Jefferson's remembrance features a poignant visual image. As a little boy, he sits
on a soft pillow, high up on a horse, cradled in the arms of another
human being. Intuitively, this pictorial impression seems fresh and
stimulating in its natural setting. The thematic focus of Jefferson's
first memory suggests an appreciation of the beauty and wonder
of beginning an exciting but largely unknown journey. There is an
elegance in his remembrance with the pillow's stylistic association
and comfort in concert with the horse evoking a sense of power and
adventure. As Jefferson is raised by one person to be received by
another this interaction elicits feelings of care and security.

The next early memory, which I refer to as the *prayer recollection*, presented different environmental conditions for Jefferson in
comparison to the pillow recollection. At the same time, there is a
congruity in both remembrances that provides a deeper grasp of Jefferson's way of being. In the prayer recollection, through a solitary
effort Jefferson employs his intellect to sustain and fortify himself.
The thematic focus of the memory relates to taking action with the
hope of changing a distressing situation. In contrast with the rich
surroundings of the pillow recollection, the prayer memory primarily emphasizes Jefferson's tactical movement and internal processing. Jefferson uses the power of his mind so that he can be free from
his adverse environment. The pillow and prayer memories draw together holistically in Jefferson's pursuit of engaging and stimulating
experiences. Another way the two memories are integrated involves
Jefferson's appreciation of the richness and aesthetic beauty in life.
When conditions fell short of his idealistic standard, Jefferson appeared to take direct action and rely upon his active mind to find
ways to enhance his existence.

Reflecting the themes of Jefferson's early recollections, an appreciation of beauty and the wonder of exploring stimulating experiences were intimately familiar to Jefferson over the course of
his eventful life. Jefferson had a readiness to take action to improve

environmental conditions and to enhance his personal development. In this regard, Jefferson's curiosity and love of learning were evident in his lifetime of study. As a college student, Jefferson claimed that he regularly studied in solitude for more than eleven hours a day.[9] Jefferson had a constant desire to master knowledge of languages, plants and fossils, star formations, and numerous other intellectual and aesthetic pursuits. In a quest for self-development, he maintained a freshness of experience by expanding the scope and breadth of his scholarly endeavors. In composing the Declaration of Independence, Jefferson applied his formidable intellectual capacities coupled with an awareness of social and political ideas from antiquity to the colonial period. In government positions that brought him to the pinnacle of fame and achievement, Jefferson constantly drew upon his depth of knowledge and exploratory yearnings. The acquisition of millions of acres of unspoiled land in the Louisiana Purchase under his presidential leadership represented his highest aspirations to explore and develop to the advantage of a new nation.

## Personality Dimensions

### Degree of Activity

In 1787, in a letter to his daughter Martha, Jefferson wrote about the importance of activity and engagement in life: "Determine never to be idle. No person will have occasion to complain of the want of time, who never loses any. It is wonderful how much may be done, if we are always doing."[10] As in his early recollections, Jefferson maintained a sense of purpose and a high degree of activity in striving toward self-fulfillment. In a life of accomplishment, Jefferson was known to rise at dawn and work sixteen-hour days. In another habitual practice, Jefferson maintained a lifelong practice of letter writing with his correspondence to friends, relatives, and associates numbering about eighteen thousand letters.[11] Jefferson enjoyed various comforts and efficiencies in life, yet he was also passionate about cultivating his capacities and maximizing his potential.

In more than two decades of public service that culminated in the presidency of the United States, Jefferson pursued lofty goals, but was also practical and disciplined. As in his first memories, Jefferson maintained broad perspectives, while simultaneously absorbing himself in intricate details. For instance, during the process of designing the sweeping scope of Monticello, Jefferson kept meticulous data on the thousands of plants that grew on the plantation.[12] Even in his retirement at Monticello, when he was in his seventies, Jefferson assumed a key role in creating the University of Virginia. This commitment by Jefferson involved him in such details as selecting faculty, determining academic courses, and establishing rules regarding student conduct.[13]

## Social Interest

In an expression of social interest, Jefferson contributed to the advancement of humanity through his extraordinary public service. As in his pillow recollection, Jefferson felt a kinship with other living beings and expressions of nature. In the American experiment, Jefferson saw an opportunity to protect individual rights and freedoms through an enlightened government and society. From a moral perspective, Jefferson thought that the well-being of people was best served through the general interest of the majority of individuals.[14] The compassion that Jefferson felt toward others was particularly evident in the devotion and nurturance he demonstrated toward his family members and close associates. In a contrasting direction that is recognizable in his prayer recollection, Jefferson had a tendency to detach himself from other people and find solace in solitary activity. In these instances, Jefferson engaged in an internal way of being through such functions as studying and personal reflection. Although Jefferson was sensitive to the practical needs of humanity, he also lived a life of privilege from childhood that included having an enslaved person as a personal attendant.[15] Looking back to some accounts of Jefferson's pillow recollection, he was made comfortable by slaves as he began his journey to Tuckahoe.[16] Jefferson was a slave owner throughout his adult life, as the labor that the slaves provided contributed to the patrician existence that he and his family enjoyed. Yet, Jefferson denounced slavery and its transgressions against humanity. Unlike, however, some other large plantation owners of his era, Jefferson did not take the step to free his slaves during his lifetime. At the same time, Virginia law and Jefferson's heavy debts toward the end of his life complicated the prospect of freeing his slaves.[17]

## Optimism/Pessimism

Jefferson's first memories reflect an optimistic outlook on life. The pillow recollection portrays the stimulation and comfort of a new experience and suggests an intrinsic level of optimism and happiness. In the prayer recollection, Jefferson utilizes his intellectual power to tolerate an unpleasant situation. Jefferson's optimism had an idealistic quality, so when reality did not meet his expectations he tended to pursue actions or engage his mind to minimize disappointment and effect more congenial conditions. In a 1787 letter to his daughter, Martha, Jefferson wrote about the relationship between engagement and happiness in life. "A mind always employed is always happy. This is the true secret, the grand recipe, for felicity. The idle are the only wretched."[18] Jefferson went on in the letter to state how the world offers many ways to usefully employ and amuse oneself in a manner which contributes to the enjoyment of life. Even when Jefferson encountered difficult circumstances, such as an exhaustion at the end of his second presidential term, he maintained expectations for better times in the future. When his public career ended, Jefferson looked forward to his retirement at Monticello to be with his family on the land that he loved. However, soon after Jefferson returned to Monticello he realized that the plantation was in serious debt. Acting to improve the financial condition of Monticello, Jefferson sold his personal library of books to Congress. Yet, even this drastic and painful move did not bring about fiscal stability. Near the end of his life with his indebtedness mounting, in one of his last efforts to save Monticello for his family, Jefferson gave approval to conduct a lottery to sell off some of the land.[19] In spite of the looming burden of debt, Jefferson was able to find domestic tranquility at Monticello through his daily horseback rides, tending to the gardens, and playing with his grandchildren. Additionally, in the final years of his life, Jefferson maintained his constant letter writing and pursued the creation of the University of Virginia.

## *Self-Efficacy*

Self-efficacy is evident in Thomas Jefferson's prayer recollection as he copes with a stressful event. In a purposeful way, Jefferson exercises personal control in managing adversity by attempting to expedite time. Unlike the pillow recollection where Jefferson experiences a positive interaction, in the prayer memory he creatively calls upon his internal resources to surmount a perceived obstacle. Jefferson appreciated enriching and stimulating experiences in life, and when confronted with challenges he would deliberately attempt to improve unfavorable situations. Although Jefferson enjoyed being surrounded by living conditions characterized by an aesthetic beauty, he also encountered numerous personal and professional misfortunes. Throughout his married life, untimely deaths within his family shook Jefferson's world and his resolve to persevere. He helplessly observed his beloved wife Martha die while delivering a baby, in addition to five of his six children dying at young ages. Politically, Jefferson dealt with rigors and problems inherent in his tenure in the nation's highest public offices for more than two decades. In his second term as president of the United States, Jefferson's decision to impose a trade embargo with England and France was highly unpopular and undermined his leadership ability.[20] Although he felt exhausted and expressed a strong desire to be free of daunting national responsibilities,

Jefferson continued to manage obligations until he completed his second term as president. He believed in his own ability and the capacities of people to draw from innate resources to persevere and flourish in life. In a 1763 letter to John Page, Jefferson wrote "Perfect happiness I believe was never intended by the deity to be the lot of anyone of his creatures in the world; but that he has very much put in our power the nearness of our approaches to it, is what I steadfastly believe."[21]

## Conscientiousness

In Jefferson's prayer recollection he uses his intellect to accelerate the time for school to be dismissed. Through this devotional act, Jefferson demonstrated a responsible and planful approach to managing a stressful situation. As another aspect of conscientiousness, Jefferson persisted in repeating the Lord's Prayer in the remembrance as an exercise of self-control. Jefferson's pillow recollection reflects conscientiousness to the extent that he is responsible in cooperating with his caretakers. Whether it was his lifelong commitment to education and self-development, dedication to ethical principles in public office, devotion to family members and friends, or dutifully paying frequent debts, Jefferson was persistent in meeting obligations and responsibilities. At the same time, Jefferson's pursuit of the good life with its inherent financial costs periodically exceeded his ability to pay his bills. In these instances, Jefferson would continue to act upon his aesthetic sensitivities while struggling to meet fiscal commitments. The idyllic existence exemplified in his pillow recollection was expensive to maintain as a way of life, and the personal restraint implied in the prayer recollection only went so far. Jefferson enjoyed a degree of luxury wherever he lived, and at times his pursuit of beautiful surroundings and lavish furnishings in his dwellings outpaced his monetary resources. As president, Jefferson incurred a significant debt, and stated that he "was leaving office with hands as clean as they are empty."[22]

## Perceptual Modalities

*Senses*

Thomas Jefferson's first memories involved multiple sensory trends including visual, auditory, and touch modalities. In the pillow recollection, vision and touch are apparent as Jefferson was lifted up to go for a ride on a horse. A visual image clearly emerges in Jefferson's prayer recollection coupled with his internal verbalization. Jefferson's early recollections do not include smell or taste representations. In Jefferson's life, his visual capacity was crucial for the pursuits of reading, architecture, landscape design, and various other activities. Auditory expressions were manifest in Jefferson's lifetime enjoyment of playing the violin and in his tendency to spend time alone to internally process his thoughts. Jefferson's sense of touch was notable in such activities as riding his horse on a daily basis, collecting thousands of books and plant species, as well as manipulating pen, ink, and paper in composing thousands of letters.

*Color*

Jefferson did not make reference to color in his early recollections. Although he had an appreciation of color in nature and in human endeavors, color was not life-orienting for Jefferson.

*Place*

Jefferson's early recollections epitomize the significance of place as a perceptual modality. The settings of Jefferson's remembrances are prominent and distinct. In the pillow recollection the woodland location is rich and evocative, and his prayer recollection enables Jefferson to find a place of solitude to actively engage his mind. In both early memories, Jefferson experienced an emotional relationship with a place that fully occupies his sensibilities. In Jefferson's life he had an orientation to place that prompted him to yearn for and seek out particular surroundings for their inspirational and aesthetic qualities. More than any other setting on earth, Monticello placed at Jefferson's disposal life-enhancing opportunities for repose and self-expression. When Jefferson was away from Monticello for extended periods he had a yearning for the plantation and its resonance of being at home. This sense of place was apparent in Jefferson's deep affection for Monticello, and with his passion for nature and a contemplative disposition, the Virginia plantation bestowed on him an ideal location. At Monticello, Jefferson was able to construct both natural and built environments in a comfortable yet elegant style. In particular, his vast gardens and stately mansion presented sources of endless interest and activity for Jefferson. The importance of the physical realm to the place-minded Jefferson also reached fruition with his conception of the University of Virginia. Jefferson was fully engaged in developing the physical geography and architectural design of the university in a way that was energizing for the aged man.

## Objects

In Jefferson's pillow recollection, the pillow is conspicuous as an item of comfort for the young child. As a living object, the horse represents a vehicle for transportation and adventure that Jefferson would continue to enjoy into his eighties. In his prayer recollection, Jefferson makes reference to a school and a house, but these particulars assume a secondary or incidental role. Throughout his life, Jefferson had an interest in material objects that served a utilitarian function or offered a measure of convenience. Objects for Jefferson evoked an even more special appeal when beauty and style were intrinsic to the pieces. Perhaps the most elegant and meaningful items that Jefferson collected were his prized books. In an 1815 letter to John Adams, Jefferson wrote "I can not live without my books."[23] In 1776, Jefferson commissioned a skilled carpenter to construct a writing desk and acquired a Windsor chair to be comfortable while composing the Declaration of Independence.[24] At Monticello, the object-minded Jefferson collected thousands of specimens of fossils, flowers, and plants. Jefferson also created elaborate instruments to measure the weather and an intricate clock that today still occupies the front hall in the mansion.

## THE LIFE AND EARLY
## RECOLLECTION OF ALBERT EINSTEIN

Born in 1879, Albert Einstein grew up in Munich in southern Germany. After graduating from college he worked in a Swiss patent office as a patent officer. During the seven years in this relatively indistinct position, Einstein devoted himself far beyond his working hours to research in theoretical physics. In an extraordinary intellectual effort, he produced several epoch-making publications, including a paper on the theory of relativity.[25] With his scientific acclaim increasing, he left the patent office and accepted an appointment as a professor at the University of Zurich, where he had received his doctorate. Throughout his career Einstein demonstrated a passion for scientific inquiry with a childlike sense of awe and wonder for solving problems.[26] In 1913, as a married father of two boys, Einstein was invited to assume a prestigious position as a professor at the University of Berlin.

During the next twenty years, Einstein became world renowned for his revolutionary theories, including his general theory of relativity and popular works. He also divorced his first wife and later remarried during this period. Einstein was recognized for his scientific achievements in 1923 when he traveled to Stockholm to receive the Nobel Prize. With Einstein's fame on the rise, people became fascinated by his towering intellect, unassuming manner, and bemused sense of detachment. With the threat of war imminent in Europe, Einstein immigrated to the United States to begin an appointment at the Institute of Advanced Study at Princeton University. In his later years, Einstein dedicated himself to speaking out against repressive human conditions and pursuing causes involving social justice and civil liberties.[27] He remained at Princeton as a celebrated world figure until his death in 1955.

With slight variations in their renderings, several published accounts exist that describe Einstein's first childhood memory. In Einstein's autobiographical notes he recounted the following early recollection:

> A wonder of such nature I experienced as a child of 4 or 5 years, when my father showed me a compass. This needle behaved in such a determined way that did not at all fit into the nature of events, which could find a place in the unconscious world of concepts (effect connected with direct "touch"). I can still remember—or at least I believe I can remember—that this experience made a deep and lasting impression on me.[28]

## AN INTERPRETATION OF ALBERT EINSTEIN'S EARLY RECOLLECTION

### Core Theme

In Albert Einstein's first memory, he experiences feelings of awe and wonder in reaction to the unanticipated compass movements. His remembrance involves a sense of mystery and curiosity about the phenomena of nature. It was inexplicable to Einstein that the needle of the compass did not conform to how events are supposed to occur in the physical realm of life. The observations of a natural condition left him perplexed but also highly intrigued. The theme of Einstein's early recollection relates to the joy of discovery and the power of the imagination. For Einstein, the novel idea of why the compass needle pointed north and the question of a magnetic field were challenges to pursue with passion and creativity.[29]

Various aspects of Einstein's intellectual and professional life are reflected in the core theme of his early recollection. Like many other scientists, he demonstrated a curiosity and commitment to solve complex problems. Throughout his life, Einstein experienced a childlike joy and even rapture in striving to unravel the mysteries of existence. In this regard, Einstein wrote, "The most beautiful experience we can have is the mysterious. It is the fundamental emotion which stands at the cradle of true art and true science."[30] Einstein had a capacity to find delight in scientific theorizing and challenging projects that captured his imagination. His theory of relativity was groundbreaking in the world of physics, and he was relentless throughout his adult life in trying to discover a unifying field theory. Einstein would frequently marvel at experiences and events in life that other people often took for granted or would simply overlook. He also had an ability, as he showed in his early childhood memory, to fully concentrate on absorbing tasks and avoid the distractions of external circumstances.

## Personality Dimensions

### Degree of Activity

For most of Einstein's life he pursued stimulating challenges and opportunities to engage his prodigious mind. As he did in his early recollection, Einstein constantly seemed to be working on some endeavor or puzzle that he found captivating. In this regard, he wrote, "Life is like riding a bicycle. To keep your balance you must keep moving."[31] Demonstrating a high degree of activity, Einstein frequently blended his passion for scientific thinking with everyday activities and interests. As an example, he enjoyed sailing a small boat and drifting aimlessly for hours in solitude as he retreated into his own reveries and theoretical thought.[32] Even though Einstein's unassuming sense of detachment and manner projected a tranquil way of being, for decades he maintained a demanding schedule of research, writing, and public appearances. Early in his academic career while developing revolutionary theories he stopped giving lectures, skipped meals, and survived on only a few hours of sleep at night. As a consequence of this grueling regimen and exhausting pace, Einstein developed a stomach ulcer and experienced an extended period of depression.[33] In a contrasting direction, Einstein appreciated simple activities in life, such as riding a bicycle, going for walks, and watching movies. However, he often gave priority to goals with a larger purpose involving a scientific mission. Even in the last hours of his life, Einstein scribbled field equations in a notebook he kept by his bedside.[34]

## Social Interest

Similar to the context of his first memory, Einstein had a tendency to detach himself from others and pursue solitary activities, but he also relished the intellectual stimulation and the camaraderie of social engagements. Einstein acknowledged that his primary interest was in the objective realm of scientific endeavors, while his ability to empathize with the feelings and hardships of people close to him was less of a strength. At the same time, Einstein felt an intimate bond with humanity, and he was sensitive to the needs of people in general. He thought that the foundation of morality was to transcend selfish concerns and to live in a way that was of service to other individuals. As a path for a moral life, Einstein wrote, "Use for yourself little, but give to others much."[35] In an observation that captures the sense of belonging and emotional bond inherent in social interest, Einstein states: "People who live in a society, enjoy looking into each other's eyes, who share their troubles, who focus their efforts on what is important to them and find this joyful—these people lead a full life."[36] Einstein frequently expressed compassion and tolerance for people through his writings and personal activism. He used his fame as a platform to speak out against repressive human conditions and the critical importance of striving for social justice and individual freedom.

## Optimism/Pessimism

In 1949, in a letter to his friend and fellow physicist, Max Born, Einstein spoke directly about his temperament. The correspondence conveys an optimistic outlook on life that is evident in Einstein's first memory. "I simply enjoy giving more than receiving in every respect, do not take myself nor the doings of the masses seriously, am not ashamed of my weaknesses and vices, and naturally take things as they come with equanimity and humor."[37] Einstein's sense of optimism is apparent as he readily acknowledges his weaknesses coupled with a tolerant and lighthearted approach to life. What Einstein did not emphasize in this self-characterization, however, was his persistent pattern of seeking out creative and absorbing tasks that brought him pleasure and fulfillment. As in his early recollection, Einstein seemed most content when engaged in stimulating and challenging pursuits. Einstein had a zest for life that enabled him to find satisfaction and meaning in simple activities and long-term consequential projects and problems. As an example, Einstein enjoyed the visual task of solving puzzles as a hobby throughout the decades that he worked on complex intellectual endeavors.

## Self-Efficacy

In his first memory, Einstein is intrigued and perplexed by the movement of the needle of the compass, and yet he persists in trying to make sense of the workings of the instrument. Throughout his life, Einstein also set high intellectual goals and committed himself to surmounting difficult and stimulating challenges. He had a belief in his capabilities and tended to persevere in spite of perceived obstacles. For instance, after graduating from college, Einstein had difficulty finding work and accepted an entry-level position. During the seven years of his day job as a Swiss patent officer, Einstein worked evenings and weekends, while producing renowned scientific papers that led to his appointment as a university professor. Through a largely solitary effort and with minimal encouragement from other scholars, Einstein was tenacious in establishing his reputation as an eminent scientist. When approaching challenging tasks and responsibilities, Einstein managed stress through private escapes and absorbing diversions. Even after decades of demanding research and strong criticism from the scientific community, he did not abandon his goal to discover a theory that would unify all the laws of the universe. This pursuit, however, would eventually end in failure despite his determination and effort.

## Conscientiousness

With an intensity that was evident in his early recollection, Einstein was diligent and self-disciplined in striving to solve scientific problems and make a difference in life. As a physicist, he committed himself to finding answers to ambitious and perplexing questions. Work for Einstein represented not only a search for substance and meaning in life, but also a means of diverting himself from difficulties in other aspects of living. In this regard, Einstein wrote, "Strenuous intellectual work and looking at God's nature are reconciling, fortifying yet relentlessly strict angels that shall lead me through all sorts of life's troubles."[38] When confronting adversities and sorrows, Einstein would find relief and solace in his scientific pursuits. At the same time, Einstein's persistence in his intellectual mission could be at odds with his commitments to family members and social conventions. As an example, although Einstein was a loving father to his two children, his professional schedule coupled with solitary and personal diversions limited his physical and emotional access to family members.

## Perceptual Modalities

### Senses

Albert Einstein's visual sense is dominant in his early recollection in comparison to his other sensory modalities. In his life, visual images and mental pictures were intrinsic to his thought processes. In an interview just before he turned fifty years old, the visually minded Einstein states: "I very rarely think in words at all. A thought comes, and I may try to express it in words afterwards."[39] An essential aspect of Einstein's visual thinking was the engagement of his imagination. Similar to the way that he visualized natural forces moving the needle in his early recollection, Einstein imagined falling elevators, lightning strikes, and moving trains in his thought experiments. Engaging such pursuits, Einstein creatively extended the capacity of his thinking through the power of imagination. In this regard, Einstein says, "Imagination is more important than knowledge. Knowledge is limited. Imagination encircles the world."[40] Even in understanding formulas in mathematics, Einstein was able to visualize a physical reality and content instead of abstract concepts. With respect to senses beyond vision, Einstein's early recollection occurs in silence, suggesting a lessened prominence of his auditory channel. At the same time, Einstein loved music and enjoyed playing the violin in his later years. In his first memory, Einstein touches the compass, and as a physicist he had frequent contact with scientific instruments. Representations of smell and taste do not occur in his early recollection, as the modalities were not life-orienting for Einstein.

*Color*

Einstein's early recollection is absent of color, as he did not manifest particular sensitivities of an artist. Yet, Einstein appreciated beauty in his elegant scientific theorizing, and through an essential simplicity in his approach to life.

*Place*

The location in Einstein's first memory is vague and somewhat incidental. The secondary nature of the setting suggests a tendency of Einstein to detach himself from his physical and social environment. Einstein's satisfaction and sense of well-being in life seemed to relate more to the richness of his internal engagement than to particular locales. To this point, Einstein reflects, "I am truly a 'lone traveler' and have never belonged to my country, my home, my friends, or even my immediate family, with my whole heart; in the face of all these ties, I have never lost a sense of distance and a need for solitude."[41]

## Objects

In Einstein's first remembrance, the compass is conspicuous and distinct, as he is enthralled by its mysterious workings. When Einstein described the operation of the compass, he primarily spoke about the allure of its functions rather than its physical features. In a similar way, throughout his life, Einstein found the most satisfaction in objects or items that could more fully captivate and engage his intellect and passions. Whether it was a puzzle, a small sailboat, a violin, or a scientific instrument, Einstein gravitated to engrossing yet simple objects. He also seemed averse to acquiring too many possessions and material things that might restrict his freedom or engender excessive comfort and complacency. One small example of this desire to avoid confining and restrictive objects was Einstein's preference to avoid wearing socks.

## THE LIFE AND EARLY
## RECOLLECTION OF MOTHER TERESA

Agnes Gonxha was born in Skopje, Serbia, in 1910, decades before becoming the acclaimed Mother Teresa. As the youngest of three children, Agnes grew up in a family and a parish community that fostered compassion and charity towards the poor and less fortunate.[42] Joining the Order of Loreto Nuns in 1928, Agnes arrived a year later in Calcutta, India to live in a convent. Within two years, she professed her religious vows of poverty, chastity, and obedience as a Sister of Loreto in the Roman Catholic Church. Serving primarily as a school teacher, Sister Teresa committed herself to a religious vocation. However, on a train journey in 1946 things changed abruptly when she heard a call from God to serve the poorest of the poor by living among them in the slums of Calcutta.[43] With scant resources amid impoverished conditions, Sister Teresa received approval from the Vatican to establish the Missionaries of Charity in 1950. As foundress of the religious order and leader to a small group of ten nuns, she became Mother Teresa. Making a deliberate choice to live among the outcasts of society, the sisters provided free services in nursing the sick, tending to the dying, and assisting the abandoned.[44]

Over the years, Mother Teresa expanded the mission of the order in hopes of serving more people on the margins of life. Sufferers with leprosy and later AIDS were of particular concern to her and the Missionaries of Charity.[45] At the same time, Mother Teresa was gaining public recognition for her dedication to the destitute in addition to her humble and unpretentious manner. The religious order expanded on a worldwide basis to include missionary sites in Caracas, Melbourne, London, Rome, and New York City.[46] The order flourished with hundreds of sisters and brothers joining the mission as Mother Teresa's reputation continued to flourish. In 1979, she was awarded the Nobel Peace Prize in Oslo for her work with the "unwanted, unloved, and uncared for."[47] Although Mother Teresa was the head of a spiritual community, she continued her daily commitment to personally tending to the downtrodden and powerless. Holding abandoned babies, treating the wounds of the dying, and even cleaning toilets were tasks intimately familiar to Mother Teresa. In spite of suffering from a heart condition that required hospitalization and experiencing a crisis of faith in her spiritual life, Mother Teresa maintained an exhausting pace involving world travel, personal appearances, and administrative responsibilities. For many years she personally responded to frequent correspondence through brief notes and letters. With her health failing Mother Teresa continued to work into her eighties, until her death due to heart failure in 1997.[48]

In the context of discussing the toxic and infectious effect of criticism by one individual in a small group of people, Mother Teresa recounts the following early recollection. "When we were little children my mother wanted to teach us what bad company does, so she bought a basket of apples, amongst which she intentionally put a bad apple. After a few days, she called us around the basket and we saw [that] all the apples, which had been beautiful a few days before, had gone bad. She then explained how one bad apple contaminated all the others. In the same way, bad companions can harm others."[49]

## AN INTERPRETATION OF
## MOTHER TERESA'S EARLY RECOLLECTION

### Core Theme

There is a straightforward and a moral tone to Mother Teresa's first memory as she intently listens to her mother make an instructive point about the importance of the company you keep. Mother Teresa's own mother gathered her family together to demonstrate how quickly something beautiful can be corrupted by harmful influences. The core theme of Mother Teresa's early recollection emphasizes a spiritual and life lesson delivered by a devout family leader. Mother Teresa was captivated by the sequence of events that took place over a period of several days. The memory also provides insight into Mother Teresa's closely knit family life in establishing an environment that was conducive to the development of faith and moral sensitivity.[50]

The core theme of Mother Teresa's early memory reflects aspects of her spiritual life and service to humanity. She assumed the responsibilities of the head of a faith community, much like her own mother did in her first remembrance. Although Mother Teresa expanded her apostolic function on a far broader scale in comparison to her mother, she maintained a similar role as an authority figure. The devout and pious quality of the remembrance is evident in her dedication to a religious vocation for more than sixty years. In much the same way that Mother Teresa was influenced by a moral lesson in her first memory, she wholeheartedly attempted to teach the value of living a life of care and kindness. Mother Teresa saw beauty and potential in the most desolate and deprived individuals, and she deeply believed that a lack of love and tolerance for the poor contaminates the spiritual and community life of all people.

## Personality Dimensions

### Degree of Activity

Spending most of her life in a religious order, Mother Teresa demonstrated a high degree of activity and dedication to humanity and a spiritual life. For decades, she awoke each morning at 4:40 a.m. to begin her day with morning prayers and a visit to the chapel. With a problem-solving focus in helping the destitute, the intense demands of the immediate moment kept her attention centered on the present rather than becoming unduly concerned about the past or even the future.[51] Consistent with the deliberate action in her early recollection, Mother Teresa gave emphasis to simple tasks that she accomplished with care and attention to the smallest detail. She saw her humble deeds of providing practical aid, affection, and advice, or expressing a smile as an opportunity to impart acts of love on the outcasts of society. In this regard, Mother Teresa relates, "Don't look for big things, just do small things with great love."[52] After Mother Teresa became famous, she was criticized for not doing more to pursue political and systemic solutions to worldwide problems of poverty. She recognized, however, that her strengths and natural capacities were more in the realm of meeting the needs of individual sufferers. As the head of an international organization, much of Mother Teresa's time was also consumed by travel obligations, public appearances, and face-to-face meetings with the religious of the Missionaries of Charity. In her immediate personal contacts, Mother Teresa saw the divine presence of Christ in each individual. Wearing a plain white sari with blue stripes, her strong-jawed and weathered face radiated a sense of joy, vitality, and peace.

## Social Interest

Through a purposeful life that is compatible with the moral theme and sense of belonging in her early recollection, Mother Teresa's compassion toward the outcasts of society found its fullest expression in her service to the poorest of the poor. Coupled with a desire to belong to a community, Mother Teresa's empathic way of being epitomized a high level of social interest. The need to love and be loved was intrinsic to Mother Teresa's nature and her affinity with humanity. Regarding this, Mother Teresa says, "Abandonment is an awful poverty. There are poor people everywhere, but the deepest poverty is not being loved."[53] Her quest to serve the abandoned and destitute led Mother Teresa to encounter people living in some of the most desperate and deprived conditions in the world. She also expanded her view of poverty to include an emptiness of spirituality and a hunger for love that tends to occur in more affluent countries. In attempting to address the vast dimensions of material, social, and spiritual poverty, Mother Teresa expanded the reach of the Missionaries of Charity across the globe. Although her efforts were challenging and demanding, she also experienced a sense of gratification and meaning in her support of the suffering. With respect to helping others, Mother Teresa stated, "Never be afraid of giving. There is a deep joy in giving. Since what we receive is much more than what we give."[54]

## Optimism/Pessimism

For most of her adult life, Mother Teresa witnessed oppressive environmental conditions and the constant degradation of human beings. Yet, in spite of the daunting hardships that she encountered on a daily basis, Mother Teresa did not become despondent or overwhelmed by the gravity of her sacred mission. Instead, she typically went about her work of service with enthusiasm and a radiant smile. At the same time, Mother Teresa made a deliberate and prayerful effort to maintain a joyful and optimistic outlook. Calling to mind the potential influence of people on one another that was a point of emphasis in her early memory, Mother Teresa states, "Joy is very contagious. Try, therefore, to always be overflowing with joy wherever you go."[55] Although she recognized that joy is not a simple matter of temperament and that it is difficult to remain joyful, Mother Teresa thought that it is essential to try to cultivate a sense of joy in life. For a period of decades, Mother Teresa endured a crisis of faith where she experienced anguished doubts about the meaning and value of her work and the existence of God.[56] Although this interior darkness and spiritual dryness was highly distressing to her, she continued to express an outward sense of optimism and a zest for life. Mother Teresa maintained an expectation for success as she tenaciously pursued an expansion of the religious and charitable work of the Missionaries of Charity throughout the world. Her optimism was also fueled by a willingness to work hard and a keen sense of reality in attempting to help people who had been abandoned by society.

*Self-Efficacy*

Anticipating success and attempting to overcome adversities represented a way of life for Mother Teresa. Similar to the theme of her early recollection, she set high expectations for herself and others. Once she established a course of action, Mother Teresa would follow through on her commitments with a fierce determination. In 1948, when she began her mission in Calcutta, Mother Teresa entered the slums of the city on a solitary journey with a meager sum of money.[57] As the Missionaries of Charity sought to expand its mission, Mother Teresa regularly encountered financial and bureaucratic challenges. In response, the diminutive nun repeatedly stood up to powerful political and institutional leaders and obstacles that hindered her quest to serve the destitute. Starting in the 1950s and continuing for almost thirty years, Mother Teresa experienced tormenting thoughts relating to her purpose in life and her relationship with Christ. With persistent doubts about her faith, she suffered from excruciating distress.[58] Throughout this dark period, however, Mother Teresa maintained a focus on her service to the impoverished and did not give in to confusion and discouragement. She also found relief from stress by seeking out advice from her religious superiors and through her constant prayer activity. Mother Teresa also possessed a keen sense of humor coupled with a humble and self-effacing manner.

## Conscientiousness

With humility and steady diligence, Mother Teresa provided tireless service to people in need over the course of her long life. Although she rarely took credit for her accomplishments, Mother Teresa's persistence and assumption of responsibility provided support to the destitute and inspired countless people to be more sensitive to the poor and abandoned. Reflecting the moral and apostolic focus of her early recollection, Mother Teresa's industry and inspirational capacities contributed to the formation of the Missionaries of Charity and the recruitment of thousands of the order's religious and volunteer workers. Her high level of conscientiousness always had a practical focus in helping individuals. As an example, essential support facilities such as soup kitchens, orphanages, and AIDS hospices were established by the Missionaries of Charity. Yet, even though the organizational structure of the mission expanded globally, Mother Teresa sought to maintain face-to-face contact with people. Similar to the interpersonal exchange found in her first memory, Mother Teresa's offering of personal and spiritual advice to the religious in the orders and spending time with the suffering was a priority for her. At the same time, maintaining an exhausting schedule compromised her health, regardless of the effort that she made to be organized. It was customary for Mother Teresa to end each of her days tending to a large amount of correspondence.[59] In 1992, I sent a note to Mother Teresa asking her to recount an early recollection and respond to follow-up questions. She acknowledged my request in the following

+LDM

1st December, 1992
MISSIONARIES OF CHARITY
54, A, A U C Bose Road
Calcutta · 700016. India

Dear Arthur Clark

Thank you very much for your letter.

I want very much people to come to know
God, to love Him, to serve Him, for that
is true happiness. And what I have I
want everyone in the world to have. But
it is their choice. If they have seen
the light they can follow it, I cannot
give them the light: I can only give the
means.

Since our work is with the Poorest of the
Poor I will not have time to answer these
questions. But please be assured of my
prayers for you that you make your life
something truly beautiful for God by
being God's love and His presence in
their lives.

God Bless you

*lu Teresa mc*

**Figure 9.1.**

letter from the Mother House of the Missionaries of Charity, and her words continue to be an inspiration to me.

## Perceptual Modalities

### Sensory

Like most people, Mother Teresa's visual channel was dominant as a sensory trend. The pictorial image of her mother demonstrating the contamination of the apples to her children is easy to visualize. Mother Teresa constantly called upon her faculty of sight to negotiate and appreciate life in all of its dimensions. In her frequent personal contacts, her visual capacity enabled Mother Teresa to empathize with a diverse range of people. In one example, Mother Teresa says, "I have looked into the eyes of children—some shining with hunger, some dull and vacant with pain."[60] In another instance, she relates, "The other day I went into the street there [in Japan]. . . . I saw a man across the street completely lost. It is true that he was drunk, but he is my brother. My brother. It hurt me."[61] Beyond vision, Mother Teresa's auditory channel was also notable in her early recollection and in her life. In Mother Teresa's first memory she listened to her mother explain the importance of keeping good company. Verbal communication was life-orienting for Mother Teresa in the form of prayer, social relationships, and her love of music. She especially enjoyed singing and playing the mandolin and was fluent in Albanian, English, and Hindi.[62] Touch as a sensory modality also had a bearing in Mother Teresa's first memory as she repeatedly called upon her sense of touch. From holding countless babies in her arms to tending to the sick and dying, Mother Teresa's human touch provided consistent comfort and love. Representations of smell and taste were not present in her early recollection. The modalities lacked a compelling quality for Mother Teresa.

### Color

Similar to smell and taste, Mother Teresa does not make reference to color in her first memory. Consequently, color is not considered life-orienting for Mother Teresa.

## *Place*

Most likely, Mother Teresa's home was the setting for her early recollection. Although she left her house and family to pursue a vocation as a nun, Mother Teresa created a home-like atmosphere through the Missionaries of Charity by establishing a nurturing and supportive environment for the religious and for whom they served. She believed that the home offers a place for family members to give and receive love. At the same time, Mother Teresa recognized that in the home and community it is easy to become indifferent to or ignore individuals who are in need of understanding or attention. Relating to this poverty of love, Mother Teresa states, "This is what we must know, do we really know that in our own family, maybe there is my brother, my sister, my wife, my husband, who feels unwanted, unloved, exhausted, looking for little compassion, little sympathy and I have no time."[63]

## *Objects*

In Mother Teresa's early memory, although the apples were captivating as tangible items, they did not represent objects that she had a desire to possess. Instead, the apples served as a vehicle to convey a moral lesson. As a nun, Mother Teresa professed a vow of poverty in which she promised to relinquish the pursuit of a material life. At the same time, she appreciated the enjoyment and aesthetic qualities that objects provide in the world. To this point, Mother Teresa states, "By nature I am sensitive, love beautiful and nice things, comfort and all the comfort can give—to love and be loved."[64] Even with this desire, however, she questioned the excessive pursuit of acquiring possessions that tends to occur in more affluent countries. Mother Teresa felt that when an individual is preoccupied with material goals, the possibility exists for neglecting human relationships and failing to contribute to those who may be suffering.[65]

*Chapter Ten*

# Making Sense of My World

## *Early Recollections in Counseling and Psychotherapy*

> Memory is not just the imprint of the past time upon us; it is the keeper of what is meaningful for our deepest hopes and fears.
>
> —Rollo May[1]

One hundred years ago, Alfred Adler first used the first memories of childhood in a therapeutic setting to gain insights into individuals' unique perspectives of life and ways of being. In turn, this empathic understanding contributed to determining goals of the treatment experience and implementing strategies for effectively working with clients. As a contemporary appraisal device, early recollections continue to illuminate how clients construe life while providing a type of road map for constructive change through the counseling process. Although early recollections constitute only one of a range of assessment tools available to a counselor or psychotherapist, the projective technique offers an incisive and enlightening method for appraising personality. Since the 1930s, researchers have explored early childhood recollections of people with a broad range of emotional disorders.[2] This type of information has contributed to clarifying psychological issues of individuals who experience significant distress in their lives. Numerous studies have related patterns of first memories to disorders of mood, anxiety, eating, addiction, and other psychological conditions. Early recollections have also been therapeutically employed in diverse treatment modalities, such as couples counseling, career counseling, and counseling with clients across the life span.

## EARLY RECOLLECTIONS IN COUNSELING AND PSYCHOTHERAPY: A CASE ILLUSTRATION

I first met Marie when she came into my office on her twenty-ninth birthday. She had been referred for counseling by her family physician due to concerns of a "low-grade depression and a sense of lethargy." Knowing that it was Marie's birthday, I wished her best wishes on the occasion. Marie replied in an emotionally muted tone, "It comes around every year, so it's no big deal." In a subdued manner, Marie went on to relate that she lived with her divorced sister, Doreen, in a small apartment in the city. Marie was unhappy with her living situation, but she thought, "It would cost me too much money to live on my own, and I can be alone when I want to escape." Marie also mentioned that she had been employed as a jeweler's assistant for the past three years and worked for a man who "really knew the jewelry business." As Marie spoke, I tried to empathize with her obvious feelings of distress and discontentment. At one point, Marie said that her life seemed "empty at times." Marie further acknowledged that she was frequently irritable toward her sister, and her boss "was not that understanding." Marie also related that she only had a few friends and recently was keeping more to herself instead of going out socially. In this regard, Marie said, "didn't feel like bothering with anyone most of the time, and there wasn't much to do anyways." As our initial time together drew to a close, we agreed to meet for counseling on a weekly basis. Upon leaving, Marie stood up and said something that was inconsistent with her dejected presence: "I'm starting to feel that our meetings could help, and maybe I can get something out of them."

When Marie came into my office for our next session, she seemed even more withdrawn and distressed than in the previous week. We started talking about the logistical hardship that coming to counseling presented her. Marie said that transportation was especially difficult because she didn't own a car and the bus runs were irregular. In a halting voice, Marie stated that she was looking forward to our session early in the week, but she began having doubts because "it wouldn't change anything, so what's the point of even talking." As we discussed her concerns, I encouraged Marie to persist with the treatment even though she had reservations about its potential effectiveness. In continuing our discussion, Marie talked about her mounting feelings of irritation toward her sister, Doreen, and her dissatisfaction with work. In particular Marie was tired of Doreen repeatedly telling her to get out more often and "stop hanging around the apartment." After discussing this conflict at some length, I decided to ask Marie to complete a self-report measure of depression. When Marie finished responding to the inventory, which I later placed her in the mild to moderate level, I asked her to provide an early childhood memory.

I found it interesting that Marie became somewhat more alert and animated as she began to recount an early recollection. Marie states: "I remember looking under the Christmas tree after presents were given out by my family and we had finished eating dinner. I noticed that there were a couple of boxes which were wrapped in pretty colors, and I thought that one of them might be for me. I could read my name, but I didn't see it on the boxes after I had looked at each one. They were for someone else." When I asked Marie if there was anything else that she could recall in the memory, she said that the Christmas tree was big and with a lot of red and blue lights. In response to another follow-up question, Marie related that not finding her name on one of the boxes was the part of the memory that she remembered most. My last question addressed Marie's feelings about the most vivid part of the remembrance. In reaction to this inquiry, Marie said that she felt "let down."

In response to my request for another early recollection Marie begins, "I was in the first grade and the teacher, Miss Ripley, had us get out of our seats and line up by the blackboard. When I was standing there I noticed that some of the desks were nice and shiny, and others were kind of old. When the teacher called our names we had to go sit down where she put us. I got one of the old desks, and most of the other kids got a new one." As an additional detail relating to my follow-up question, Marie adds, "the top of my desk had black scribbles on it, and the kids sitting in the new desks were excited." The most vivid part of her remembrance was "seeing my desk and knowing that it was not a new one," and at that point Marie felt "really disappointed and upset." Marie went on to share another memory, which was similar to her other early recollections in terms of experiencing an emotional letdown toward the conclusion of the remembrances.

Immediately after I completed writing down Marie's first memories and follow-up questions, I asked her what she would like to talk about. After pausing, Marie again began to discuss issues that she had with her place of employment. Although Marie said that she enjoyed working with jewelry, and that her "boss wasn't that bad," there were few opportunities to meet other people her age. When I said something about giving consideration to seeking out social opportunities outside of work, Marie suddenly lowered her head and peered away from me. We struggled through the rest of our session together, and I felt that Marie was becoming less engaged with me as our time concluded.

During the week preceding Marie's next visit, I had an opportunity to reflect on our first two sessions and evaluate her early recollections. I thought about my suggestion that she seek out social opportunities outside of work, and I realized that my comment was less than empathic. After all, she had already told me that her sister was constantly pushing her to go out more often. Relating to Marie's first memories, from a thematic perspective each of her remembrances began on a positive note and ended with a disappointing outcome. The core theme of Marie's early recollections seemed to involve the prospect of hopeful situations degenerating to an eventual letdown.

With respect to personality dimensions, Marie appeared poised to actively engage in experiences, although they seemed to conclude in less than positive ways. Marie's social interest was reduced as she perceived that other people appeared to receive more attention or advantages in comparison to her. Considering that her expectations often ended with a discouraging result, Marie's outlook on life may be considered generally pessimistic. Relating to self-efficacy, Marie initially seems to engage in situations with a hopeful stance, but she eventually loses faith in herself and the prospect of positive outcomes. This posture possibly has the effect of diverting Marie from pursuing endeavors because her efforts often seem to conclude with disappointment and disillusionment. Similarly, in Marie's view, maintaining responsible and dutiful behavior in the form of conscientiousness does not appear to improve situations in her life regardless of her efforts.

Relating to Marie's early recollections and perceptual modalities, her visual sense was conspicuous and distinct. She was visually aware of specific details in her remembrances, and no other sensory expression was prominent. Color was also notable as Marie made reference to various hues in each of her first memories. Home and school, as locales in Marie's early recollections, assumed an adverse quality in terms of comfort or support. In each of her early recollections, Marie made reference to prominent objects, including the Christmas tree and the student desks. From a perceptual point of view, based on Marie's responses to her first memories, Marie may be considered to be visually, color, and object-minded.

To organize the insights from a client's early recollections in counseling and psychotherapy, I have found it helpful to utilize a *lifestyle syllogism*.[3] The syllogism depicts an individual's schemas or mental structures of oneself, other people, and events in life which are formed in early childhood.[4] A lifestyle syllogism may be completed through the following framework: "I am . . . ," "Others are . . . ," "Events are . . . ," and "Therefore, life is. . . ." For Marie, my selection of schemas for her lifestyle syllogism included: "I am a loser." "Others seem indifferent to me or have more than me." "Events are frequently disappointing or distressing." "Therefore, life is often futile and dismal." In addition to what I learned about Marie's personality dimensions and perceptual modalities, the rubric provided me with a framework for empathically understanding her way of being.

As we continued in counseling, my consideration of perspectives from Marie's early recollections assisted me in grasping what it is like to be her for a momentary period of time. In this regard, what is it like to believe that events in life generally result in an emotional letdown, and circumstances provide little hope for change? As we discussed various experiences that Marie encountered, I was in a more enlightened position to grasp her anticipation of disappointing outcomes. I also knew that simply prompting or exhorting Marie to attempt to change her self-defeating behavior and to show more initiative would be no match to the power of her ingrained convictions or schemas. Perhaps what was most important as I communicated my empathic understanding to Marie was that there was an enhancement of trust and rapport between us.

In time, our improved relationship enabled me to supportively challenge Marie's maladaptive convictions of life in an attempt to loosen the influence of her maladaptive schemas. At different points, I would bring to mind what I call a *prime early recollection* as an evocative way to remind myself through my imagination how difficult it is for a client to transform deep beliefs at the core level. For Marie, I would visualize her hopefully looking for a present under a Christmas tree and feeling emotionally empty when she did not find one. Over several weeks of counseling, Marie began to make some small but important gains in establishing more purposeful schemas or patterns of thinking. With the passage of more time, Marie began to soften her belief that disappointment is largely inevitable in life to something like "I can do something about making some things turn out better for me."

With Marie's movement toward more constructive perspectives in life at the core level, she began to assume an increased motivation to act in increasingly adaptive ways. Calling upon the strong visual capacity that was evident in her early recollections, Marie was able to readily visualize personal scenarios in which she would plan to pursue enjoyable activities. As an example, Marie pictured herself taking a pottery class and possibly making a social acquaintance by talking to people in the group. Utilizing Marie's personal orientation to color, which was apparent in her first memories, she decided to bring flowers and colored figurines to her work setting and place them on her desk to get an emotionally uplifting "color fix" on a daily basis. As Marie felt somewhat more certain about her ability and control to effect more positive outcomes in her life, she began to accept a few social invitations to go out. Marie had already been making jewelry designs as a hobby, and she brought several pieces of jewelry to my office and proudly showed them to me. Toward the end of our time together in counseling Marie gave me a bracelet, and she said that my appreciative reaction was almost better than finding presents under a Christmas tree.

## EARLY RECOLLECTIONS IN DIVERSE THERAPEUTIC MODALITIES

### Early Recollections in Couples Counseling

Therapeutic use of early recollections in counseling with couples goes beyond empathically understanding the way of being of two individuals. Grasping the hopes and expectations of each partner for one another is possible by reflecting on the meaning of their respective remembrances. Considering the central importance of the relationship between couples, first memories have a potential to validate why a person acts in a certain way and brings a degree of understanding to partner qualities that are found to pose difficulties for either of the individuals in the relationship. There is a growing literature that addresses the application of early recollections with couples as a resource for clarifying the values and goals of each partner and the aspirations and concerns of the couple for their relationship.[5] The use of early recollections with couples have also been found to contribute to the improvement of communication between partners and highlight strengths in their mutual interactions. As a personality appraisal tool for use with couples, early recollections complement a practitioner's behavioral observations, interviews, and other assessment methods. Case studies are often used in the professional literature for clarifying the course of treatment with couples, and the following case illustrates the therapeutic application of early recollections with a couple in counseling.

Julie and Hank came to counseling due to strains in their relationship that had led to a temporary separation between the couple. Julie met Hank in high school, and after graduating they started dating while completing degrees as licensed practical nurses. After two years, they began living together and at some point planned to be married. Julie initiated counseling because she felt that Hank had become excessively withdrawn, and, outside of sexual relations, "He hardly ever touches me." She also stated in a resentful tone that Hank spent a lot of time alone in the basement or out in the yard working on projects. Hank said that he "didn't find that much wrong between myself and Julie that was different from most couples." He did, however, feel that Julie was quick to criticize him even though he "wasn't out all hours like some guys." When the counselor asked what strengths each person brought to their relationship, Julie and Hank thought that they both were levelheaded and reliable. Julie did express a further concern about what kind of a father Hank would make because he would often cut himself off from other people. Julie and Hank also added that they liked to spend time together, but these occasions had become less frequent.

After a period of discussion in the next counseling session, the counselor, in turn, asked Julie and Hank to provide recollections from their early childhood. Julie begins, "I remember being with my mother in the kitchen of our old house and standing in front of an old wooden table. My mother used to wear a pretty apron when she was baking. On this day, she let me put it on, and it was really big. My mother tied the apron around me so that it would stay on, and we laughed and hugged each other." Julie added that she stood on a chair as she helped her mother blend a mix in a large silver bowl. The most vivid part of the remembrance for Julie was hugging her mother, and at that point she felt "cared about and special." After Julie completed her first memory, the counselor asked Hank to recall a remembrance. Hank states, "I was upstairs in my bedroom playing with a bunch of pieces of wood that were kept in a big box. I was on the floor building a fort for my toy soldiers." As additional details, Hank mentioned that the walls around the fort were high and he also made billets for the soldiers. For Hank, the most vivid part of the memory was "seeing the fort and the buildings come together with the different pieces of wood." At that moment, Hank felt "kind of proud." Before concluding the assessment, the counselor proceeded to elicit another first memory from Julie and Hank and also administered a couple's relationship inventory.

Between treatment sessions, the counselor reflected on the appraisal material conveyed by Julie and Hank, including their early recollections. From a first memories perspective, the marked differences between the core themes of the couple were apparent involving affective communication. Relating to behavioral trends, Julie seemed to find contentment from intimate and caring relationships, and Hank found solitary and engrossing hands-on tasks fulfilling. With respect to personality dimensions, the couple demonstrated patterns of notable strengths and complementary characteristics shared by both partners. Both Julie and Hank sought out activity on a regular basis, and each exhibited qualities of self-efficacy and conscientiousness. They also had a common ground in their generally optimistic outlook on life. In terms of perceptual modalities, in their everyday lives both Julie and Hank shared a prominent visual and touch orientation. However, Julie's touch preferences largely involved people, and Hank's touch tendencies were inclined more toward working with his hands in manipulating objects.

It was evident to the counselor that, even though they knew one another for several years in an intimate relationship, Julie and Hank lacked a deeper grasp of the ways of being and each other's outlook on life. Julie was frustrated about Hank's seeming unwillingness to be more emotionally present for her, and Hank saw Julie as excessively critical and demanding toward him, particularly in her need for physical contact. To begin to reconcile their differences at fundamental levels, the counselor realized that it was essential for Julie and Hank to enhance an empathic understanding of each other's perspectives and come to terms with their differences. Although Julie understandably wished to increase Hank's emotional and physical presence, recognizing Hank's ingrained tendency to seek out solitude was also necessary. At the same time, Hank needed to understand that at times his solitary pursuits were at odds with Julie's desire to be with him. Finding a way to address and work through these core differences in a respectful way would become a major goal in treatment.

In subsequent counseling sessions, Julie and Hank verbally explored their personal perspectives on life and how the views affected their relationship in positive and negative ways. In time, the couple began to make concrete behavioral changes that were predicated upon an empathic understanding of the qualities and trends of their deepest nature. As an example, Hank made a commitment to spend more time with Julie in mutually enjoyable activities and express affection through touch on a daily basis. Julie agreed to be less critical of Hank and to find ways that were agreeable to her in support of his need to spend time alone working on projects. The personality and perceptual strengths of Julie and Hank that were in part identified through their early recollections facilitated these changes, as the counselor capitalized on the couple's potentialities throughout the counseling experience.

## Early Recollections and Life Span Counseling

Challenges and demands confront individuals at different stages of life and at times therapeutic intervention in the form of counseling services may be needed to effectively manage adversities. From an assessment perspective, early recollections are one appraisal tool that clarifies a client's capacity to cope with challenging experiences across the life span. As an example, in counseling with children and adolescents, first memories have a potential to illuminate central issues relating to self-esteem and self-concept, discipline and self-regulation, academic motivation, and other key facets of functioning.[6] At the other end of the age spectrum, in late adulthood early recollections clarify a client's core convictions and ways of being when encountering difficult transitions involving loss of intimate relationships, retirement, and health concerns.[7]

## Early Recollections in Career Counseling

In another counseling focus, early recollections as a projective technique have been found to be therapeutically useful in the area of career exploration and career development.[8] Relating to vocational decision making, a basic psychological assumption is that people are more likely to find satisfaction in career fields that are compatible with ingrained personality and perceptual trends revealed in their early recollections. In other words, the personal fit of an occupation and level of performance in the position is enhanced when the nature of the work is aligned with subjective qualities and goals reflected in an individual's first memories.[9] In a somewhat humorous example relating to this premise, in the late 1970s, I worked with an adolescent in counseling who shared with me his early recollection of him sitting in a baby carriage and being wheeled around by his mother. He found the ride pleasant and enjoyable. About twenty years after our meetings, the now nearly middle-aged man came running up to me on the street. As we greeted each other, he excitedly told me that he "owned a taxi cab and loved driving it for a living!"

From another perspective, an individual's personality dimensions, such as optimism, self-efficacy, and conscientiousness, found at higher levels in early recollections, relate to desirable and valuable work habits in most occupations and contribute to vocational success.[10] At the same time, weaker personality functions revealed through early recollections and other sources are subject to growth and development when a person makes a commitment to enhance positive vocational attributes. Relating to the perceptual modalities, prominent sense and color capacities which become manifest in an individual's early recollections potentially relate to satisfaction and competency in particular types of work. A strong visual modality, for example, is prerequisite in the fields of carpentry and architecture. An orientation to the modes of place and objects, as assessed in a person's early recollections, may possibly find expression in particular career fields and occupations. Consider, for example, in a first memory an individual is walking through a wooded area in a rural setting and takes delight in the wonders of nature. In keeping with this first memory, there is a possibility that the person has an interest in occupations involving work outdoors.

Even though early recollections have a lengthy history for enhancing treatment progress in counseling and psychotherapy, the projective technique has a relatively low frequency of use in therapeutic contexts. With a contemporary emphasis on empirically based interventions in psychology, a personality device which relies on a subjective scoring system raises questions about objective accuracy and reliability. In this regard, personality inventories that provide normative data and quantitative measurement are currently more popular among practitioners in mental health settings. In addition, early recollections as a projective technique may be unfamiliar to many practitioners because they have not been introduced to the procedure in their education and training programs. Relatedly, there are a reduced number of individuals with sufficient background in early recollections who are in a position to provide effective training for professionals. What may be most important is that practical and systematic procedures for interpreting first memories have not been widely dispersed to practitioners who provide therapeutic treatment. In my professional writings on early recollections, including *Dawn of Memories*, I have attempted to address some of these concerns.

With the increasing availability of sound research and practices involving early recollections, practitioners may be more receptive to pursuing training opportunities and utilizing the assessment device in therapeutic practice. Given the complexity of mental health issues today, the employment of reputable objective and projective assessment procedures would seem to provide a more comprehensive way of knowing a client and assist in developing effective treatment plans and interventions.

Since each early recollection is unique, every remembrance of a client reveals a fresh and compelling story for a counselor or psychotherapist to hear and understand. Entering a client's world of early childhood is a privilege, even if the stay only lasts for a momentary period of time. When professionals accrue experience in eliciting and interpreting first memories, their therapeutic skill base improves not only with the projective technique but also in the critical competency of understanding people. As a personality tool that requires the direct participation of a practitioner in the early recollection interpretation process, gains in knowledge of human development and abnormal functioning never ceases. With an individual client, a deeper awareness of her pattern of life may be directly translated into empathic therapeutic interventions. In this respect, empathy is an essential process for both interpreting early recollections and as a way of knowing the client through the counseling process.[11]

*Chapter Eleven*

# Looking through
# My Eyes and Yours

## *Early Recollections in Personal Use*

In memory each of us is an artist: each of us creates.

—Patricia Hampl[1]

Every early childhood memory is unique and tells a brief but essential story about a person. Beyond listening to a vast number of client early recollections in counseling contexts, I have reflected upon the dozen or so stories that I am able to recall from the first years of my life. I have also had the opportunity to hear the first memories of my parents, my wife, and even those of our three daughters. As I thought about the meaning of my own memories and the remembrances of my family members, I believe that I gained a deeper appreciation of how each individual has perceived and navigated through life. At informal gatherings, I have had the pleasure of listening to numerous early recollections that friends and acquaintances have recounted, and invariably these interactions have led to spirited discussions on the topic of the first memories of life. Over a period of years, in giving consideration to my own early remembrances, I have been able to call upon some of my understandings to pursue more constructive actions in my life. In a similar way that exploring early recollections has enriched my personal perspectives, evaluating first memories has a potential for a broad range of individuals to increase their self-understanding and gain a fresh awareness of how other people perceive life. Guidelines for eliciting early recollections and the

*Dawn of Memories* interpretation model contribute to facilitating this endeavor.

## RENDERINGS AND MEANINGS
## OF EARLY RECOLLECTIONS IN MY LIFE

One of my first memories clearly stands out for me as a prime early recollection. I have brought this remembrance to my mind many times over a period of decades, and I evoke the same visual image on each occasion that I recall this memory. "It was the day of my First Communion, and I still had on the suit that I had worn to church that morning. My younger brother Bob and I were playing outside of the apartment building where my aunt and uncle lived in South Boston. All of a sudden, I realized that I had lost all of the money that my relatives had given me for my First Communion. I looked at Bob, but I knew that he had no idea where my money went." As an additional detail to the recollection, I remember standing near the brick building where we were playing. The most vivid part of the memory was, "looking through my pockets and realizing that all of my money was gone." At that point I felt "shocked." Even as I write about this memory, approximately sixty years after the experience, my heart still beats somewhat rapidly. The core theme of my remembrance involves the significant loss of something valuable, specifically money. Two additional first memories that I am able to recall also relate to experiencing a loss or a lack of money.

Throughout most of my life I have had a problem with money. Rarely has my concern been about having insufficient money; instead I tend to be anxious about spending cash unnecessarily or losing the money that I have in some foolish way. I would like to pick up this narrative at the point when I was in my mid-twenties working as a school counselor. At a school event I met Marybeth, a charming young schoolteacher. I asked her to go out to dinner with me to a restaurant in Boston on the following Saturday evening. After arriving at the restaurant and being seated, I glanced at the menu and thought that the meal prices were on the high side. I then decided to inform Marybeth about my fiscal concern. She seemed displeased at my comment, but we proceeded to order our dinners. A little while later, I obscrved a waiter with a white linen towel draped over his arm idly standing a few tables away from where we were sitting. At that point, I related to Marybeth, "Part of the reason why the dinner prices are kind of high is that some of the employees in the restaurant, like that waiter, are not working to their full capacity." Reacting to my observation, Marybeth said in a firm tone, "You are taking all of the fun out of our dinner."

Marybeth and I finished our meal with an underlying tension in our conversation. After leaving the restaurant and accompanying Marybeth home, I went back to my apartment and thought about how pathetic I was at dinner, and how much I liked her. Impulsively, I decided to call Marybeth, even though I had no idea what I would say to her. When she answered the telephone, her voice was chilly, and I blurted out that I was sorry for my rude and unacceptable behavior. I then admitted that I had a problem with spending money, and that I needed to do better with it. I cannot recall much more of our conversation, but Marybeth hesitatingly agreed to see me again. Before our next date, I worked on telling myself not to say anything stupid about money. As things turned out we started dating, but a few months later I had to relocate to Oklahoma to pursue further graduate studies.

Shortly after arriving in Oklahoma, I was introduced in one of my university courses to early recollections as a projective technique. In a class activity, I recalled my First Communion memory, and had an opportunity to interpret the remembrance. I was immediately struck by how much the early recollection emotionally resonated with me and seemed to capture my way of being. That night I called Marybeth on the telephone and excitedly told her about my memory and how I made sense of the remembrance. I tried to explain to her how it seemed to say something about my problem with money. Within a year, to my good fortune, Marybeth and I were married and she joined me in Oklahoma. Numerous times over the years, she has had to remind me that thinking too much about money can take the pleasure out of life for myself and the people that I love. Marybeth knows that I have struggled to follow this advice, and she has been a strong influence in helping me control and come to terms with my tendencies to be excessively frugal. I have also acknowledged my issue with money to my children and with my friends, as if it wasn't obvious to them anyway. I no longer fret and make a fuss about spending money (well, almost never) when we go to a restaurant, but I do get an emotional lift when I happen to find a coin on the street.

At one point in the first years of our married life, I asked Marybeth to relate one of her early memories. Marybeth states, "I remember my father reading to me and hearing his voice. He was sitting next to me and reading out of a large black book of children's stories. There was a breathy quality and a smooth rhythm to his voice. The characters in the stories were accompanied by black and white illustrations or woodcuts." In response to my question, Marybeth added an additional detail of sitting with her father in a large red leather chair. The most vivid part of the memory for Marybeth was hearing the words of the story as her father spoke, and at that point she felt "a sense of enjoyment, comfort, and warmth."

The thematic focus of Marybeth's early memory involves a verbal exchange in a caring and interpersonal experience. In her daily life, Marybeth especially enjoys conversations while visiting with people, and is employed as a speech pathologist. When we were first married, I remember hearing her talking in another room in our apartment. I thought that she was on the telephone with someone, but I soon realized that this was not the case. Like many other auditory-minded people, Marybeth at times verbalizes to herself when completing solitary tasks. With color in her memory, Marybeth has an orientation to color in her life. Not being color-minded, I have directly benefited from her sensitivity and attunement to color. By making reference to particular hues, Marybeth has broadened my awareness of the expansive array of colors in our visits to art museums, natural outdoor settings, and even walks around the neighborhood.

When our children, Heather, Tara, and Kayla, were around nine or ten years old I asked each of them to recall an early recollection. I was initially hesitant to inquire about their remembrances at an earlier age because it seemed a little odd for me to evaluate my daughters through the use of a personality assessment device. When the time seemed right, I asked my oldest daughter, Heather, to recall a first memory. Heather states: "I was lying on my stomach on the floor on the sun porch. I felt really warm. I could see the sun rays and dust coming out and it was very orange." Heather added a detail of seeing a wooden door. The most vivid part of the memory for her was "the warmth and the visual of physical sun rays with their orange color." Relating to the most vivid part of her remembrance, Heather felt "very content, peaceful."

The aesthetic features of Heather's early recollection are apparent beyond the arresting color imagery in her remembrance. There is a holistic aspect to her first memory that integrates Heather's visual, emotional, and visceral experiencing. The memory presents a dreamlike quality with its serene tone and sense of tranquility. The thematic core of Heather's remembrance suggests the inherent beauty of an environment for evoking contentment and serenity. Heather, now in her early thirties, has always demonstrated a strong interest in artistic endeavors and pursuits. As a child, she was constantly drawing pictures and working on art projects. Through her adolescence and beyond, Heather devoted many hours to constructing sculptures. Our house, from the basement to the attic and garage, became full of her artistic creations. With my pecuniary tendencies, I would at times wonder, "Where is all of this leading?" On more than one occasion Heather said, "I need to take a year off and do nothing but art." This made me feel uneasy when she was doing well in school or held professional positions in her field of green technology and sustainability. Yet, attuning to the meaning of Heather's early recollection helped me to react more calmly and be more understanding of her artistic quest which she found fulfilling. Today, Heather has a large studio on her property in Virginia where she is able to pursue her artwork. The other night she called me on the telephone and said, "Dad, I had the greatest day. It was nice and warm out, and I had the big door of the studio open. I was working on a sculpture and could watch the kids playing in the yard." Not only did Heather's first memory give me a deeper insight into her aesthetic sensitivities, I also acquired a better grasp of how artists perceive the world and find their place in it.

As the middle child in a family of six children, I can remember that at times it was difficult for my parents to keep us all fed. Although we grew up with scant monetary resources, none of my brothers and sisters dwell on money in the distressful way that I have shown in my life. A number of years ago, I asked my older brother, Tom, to share an early recollection because I wanted to get a better sense of how one of my siblings dealt with money. In response, Tom relates, "I remember being with my father in the living room of our old house. I had a toy pistol and holster, but I didn't have a belt that I could put them on. Dad gave me his belt, but it was far too big. I saw some newspapers nearby on the floor, and I rolled up the papers and stuffed them in my pants so that the belt would fit and stay on my waist." Tom added details of feeling the warmth of the sunlight coming in the room and seeing the stained dark woodwork. The most vivid part of his memory was "knowing that my father was sitting nearby on the sofa, not particularly looking at me. He didn't stop me from what I was doing, and I could work at my own pace." Relating to his feelings about the most vivid part of his remembrance, Tom replies, "I felt loved and supported."

The thematic core of Tom's early recollection emphasizes a resourceful and problem-solving focus. When confronted with a challenge, he seems to find a way to successfully and creatively address the difficulty. There also is an aesthetic quality to his first memory, as color is prominent. As Tom's younger brother, I remember him in high school as a class officer, yearbook editor, and class artist. He was a hard guy to try to stay up with in terms of achievement.

Yet, the most challenging competition for me occurred when Tom was becoming established in his career. He moved up quickly to senior corporate positions in advertising and became a founder and owner of his own advertisement and marketing firm. In all of these endeavors he brought his resourcefulness, problem-solving, and artistic sensitivities to their full expression. Yet with my monetary risk-aversiveness, I would begin to feel anxious when he told me about his latest commercial ventures involving fairly large financial transactions. At the same time, Tom always viewed the business deals as opportunities to grow—even those that sometimes ended in failure. When I gave full consideration to Tom's early recollection, I began to more fully understand him, in addition to shedding light on my own way of being. As he did in his first memory, he would trust in himself to adapt to varying environmental conditions and take advantage of available resources.

Exploring the early recollections of my family members has helped me to broaden my way of knowing each person. Over the years, furthering my understanding about what was most meaningful to them has helped me to be more empathic in our day-to-day interactions. Reflecting on my own first memories has deepened my self-understanding and enabled me to gain greater awareness of some of my strengths and weaknesses. In my First Communion memory, I was able to make sense of a constrictive pattern in my life relating to money that was at times distressful for myself and other people in my life. I also had the opportunity to evaluate my other first memories, and this pursuit has also been enlightening for me. Of course in interpreting the early recollections, I had the advantage of drawing from years of study and experience with the remembrances. At the same time, I believe that the insights that emerge from the employment of early recollections should be available to far more people than just the relatively small number of practitioners who currently utilize the projective technique. Although there have been other books published for the general public on the use of first memories of life, they did not emphasize the vast scholarship available on the remembrances or provide a systematic interpretation approach for early recollections.[2] In *Dawn of Memories*, I have tried to convey important findings from the literature about early recollections and their potential for enhancing self-understanding and grasping the ways of being of people from diverse backgrounds. My goal has also been to suggest the value in employing first memories for clarifying personal strengths and potential areas of growth through a clear interpretation model.

## ELICITING AND INTERPRETING EARLY RECOLLECTIONS: THE *DAWN OF MEMORIES* MODEL

Considerations for processing early recollections have been presented throughout various chapters of the text. Consolidating this information in the form of guidelines in combination with an outline of the *Dawn of Memories* model should assist in clarifying the employment of first memories for personal use. Following specific procedures potentially facilitates the pursuit of evoking one's own early recollections or eliciting remembrances from another person. Once first memories are recalled, particular steps suggest the meaning of the recollections through a framework involving core themes, personality dimensions, and perceptual modalities.

### Eliciting Early Recollections

Even though the process of calling to mind first memories seems fairly straightforward, various considerations contribute to eliciting remembrances so that they may be subject to accurate interpretations. Most often people are willing or even eager to share early recollections because they have a special interest in their own remembrances. In some cases, however, an individual may be hesitant to reveal a first memory or feel uncomfortable with the whole disclosure process. In these somewhat rare instances, it is best to avoid further prompting of the person to disclose a remembrance. Possibly another occasion may present a more opportune time for the individual to relate an early recollection.

## Age

As a projective technique, early recollections employ uniform directions in order to elicit remembrances from a person regardless of the age of an individual. With children, however, there are limitations to the degree to which a child is able to understand instructions for recalling a first memory. Most children age eight or older are capable of recounting an early recollection, while those seven years old and younger vary widely in their ability to accurately formulate and recount a memory from early childhood. "A long time ago" for a young child may relate to something that happened a few months earlier.

## Recollections versus Reports

At times, when people recall an early recollection they recount remembrances of activities or events during childhood that occurred over an extended period. Taking a Sunday drive, for example, with one's family in an automobile may have been a regular routine for a child when growing up. In contrast to this report of a repeated pattern of activity, a first memory involves a distinct episode, and this one-time experience must be differentiated from a report for interpretation purposes.

## Number

Giving consideration to a single early recollection of a person generally allows for a manageable assessment experience at a particular time. The administration and interpretation process is sufficiently complex that even one remembrance requires a concentrated effort to accurately process the remembrance. With experience in working with first memories, additional remembrances of an individual may be elicited and interpreted on a single occasion. In counseling, I have found that evaluating three early recollections of a client in counseling a single session provides a workable number of remembrances for interpretation purposes.

## Uncertainty about Feelings

Typically, individuals are able to accurately identify their feelings relating to the most vivid aspects of their first memories. Occasionally, however, some people have difficulty describing or identifying their feelings in response to this essential follow-up question. In these instances, allowing the time that may be needed to communicate one's feelings often prompts an emotional reaction. If the person after a brief period is still unable to express her feelings relating to the most vivid aspect of a remembrance, concluding the inquiry process is preferable. When interpreting the memory, consider doing so without the benefit of knowing the feelings of the individual. However, keep in mind that the omission of a feelings response to the most vivid aspect of an early recollection likely reduces a more accurate understanding of the remembrance.

## Transcribing

When eliciting an early recollection, attempting to write down a verbatim account of the remembrance and follow-up questions is a sound practice. In the absence of written material for later reference, recalling and interpreting a person's first memory with accuracy may be difficult or even impossible. Narrations of first memories, including responses to follow-up questions, are generally brief. However, at times more lengthy renditions do occur and abbreviating words is one strategy that helps keep pace with the articulation of an individual's communications.

## Directions

After introducing the idea of assessing early recollections to a person and establishing a comfortable climate for discussion, begin eliciting a remembrance by saying: "Think back to a long time ago when you were little, and try to recall one of your earliest memories, one of the first things that you can remember." When it appears that the individual has completed expressing his memory, immediately ask three follow-up questions:

1. "Is there anything else that you can recall in the memory?"
2. "What part do you remember most in the memory?"
3. "How are you feeling at that point?" or "What feelings do you remember having then?"

## Interpreting Early Recollections

When employing the *Dawn of Memories* model for interpreting early recollections, Table 11.1 provides a profile of the core themes, personality dimensions, and perceptual modalities. Reference to this rubric may be helpful in the interpretation process with individuals. A core theme clarifies the main idea or the central topic of a person's remembrance, and this thematic focus often has significant implications in the everyday life of the individual. Personality dimensions encompass five human qualities that are critical to the psychological well-being and potentialities of an individual. Perceptual modes relate to a range of faculties that provide insights into how a person perceives and engages life. Although the interpretation model distinguishes threefold aspects, there is a unity to human behavior in terms of functioning and understanding. In this regard, a person is more comprehensively understood when the ways of knowing are drawn together holistically. Chapter 5, "The Whistle," provides an overview for integrating the multiple perspective model in the context of the life of Benjamin Franklin.

### Core Themes

A key to understanding the central message of an early recollection is to give consideration to the second follow-up question. The response to this inquiry, "What part do you remember the most in the memory?" frequently pinpoints the core theme of an individual's

**Table 11.1   Dawn of Memories, An Early Recollections Interpretation Model**

- Core Themes
- Personality Dimensions
  - Degree of Activity: Initiative, persistence, and engagement in events
  - Social Interest: Compassion, cooperation, and contribution with respect to others
  - Optimistic/Pessimistic: Expectation of positive or negative events
  - Self-Efficacy: Belief in ability to surmount challenges and anticipate success
  - Conscientiousness: Responsibility, diligence, perseverance, and productivity
- Perceptual Modalities
  - Senses:
    - Vision
    - Hearing
    - Touch
    - Smell
    - Taste
  - Color
  - Place
  - Objects

remembrance. The concluding follow-up question, "How are you feeling at that point? or "What feelings do you remember having then?" often clarifies the person's emotional response or feelings relating to the essential theme of the memory. Chapter 6, "Capturing the Big Picture," presents an in-depth analysis of core themes in first memories.

## Personality Dimensions

Dimensions of personality in the early recollections model include degree of activity, social interest, optimism/pessimism, self-efficacy, and conscientiousness. The interpretation task involves estimating the relative degree to which each quality seems to emerge in an individual's first memories. Chapter 7, "Becoming a Person," comprehensively describes the personality dimensions and their qualitative representation in early recollections.

*Perceptual Modalities*

The early recollections interpretation model details perceptual modes that focus on the senses, color, place, and objects. Determining the prominence of each of the modalities in first memories contributes to understanding of how an individual perceives and engages life. Chapter 8, "I Am What I Perceive," discusses the perceptual modes and their relationship to individuals' diverse ways of being.

## FINAL THOUGHTS ON EARLY RECOLLECTIONS

We cannot choose our early childhood memories, but we can try to understand them. In a person's first years of existence, memorable images become ingrained that communicate a powerful message concerning what life is like or about. When utilizing the *Dawn of Memories* model, first memories reflect significant domains of human functioning that convey deep convictions established in the early and formative period of human development. The brief stories spoken through early recollections potentially reveal insights into aspects of life which are orienting and meaningful to individuals.

Every early recollection is unique, and each remembrance provides a potential means to grasp the individuality of a person. Many of the experiences in first memories suggest basic and fundamental understandings about humanity in terms of self-realization. Often it is the simpler and more accessible spheres of life which emerge in first memories and are most compelling to people. In this regard, individuals, as in their early recollections, frequently find satisfaction and meaning in life by seeking out the company of others or in the pursuit of engaging activities.

Many children during their early years have had the good fortune of being able to witness magnificent natural settings and the splendor of built environments. Yet, in spite of having such opportunities as viewing the ocean from a rising cliff, peering across a shimmering clear lake, or gazing down from the thirtieth floor of a city skyscraper, these are not the typical experiences found in first memories. Instead, the content of the remembrances largely consists of everyday activities and events that are not particularly memorable to anyone other than to the person who maintains the experience through memory. Instances such as playing with a special toy in one's backyard or riding a bicycle for the first time are more representative of the content of first memories. Recognizing that early recollections serve a guiding purpose in life helps explain why the remembrances are often more commonplace and somewhat simple. At the same time, although the marvelous experiences that life allows in the early years certainly impresses and influences young children, only particular events are included in the repository of first memories.

Early recollections portray unique ways of how individuals perceive life. Glimpses into these perspectives is possible by reflecting on the illuminating stories that speak from the dawn of memories. For particular people, early recollections convey personal convictions which suggest that life is stimulating or even bountiful. For these individuals, they generally find that events in life are positive and satisfying. In the case of some other persons, their first memories involve burdensome or possibly bleak images, therefore experiences in life seem to be far less satisfying. Yet, even for individuals with distressful or disturbing early recollections, ingrained personal qualities and perspectives revealed in the remembrances are subject to the prospect of change and development. Regardless of the unique nature of the ways of being revealed through first memories, all people share in a universal potential for growth in life.

# Notes

## CHAPTER 1

1. Baldwin, *One to One*, 68.
2. Clark, *Early Recollections: Theory and Practice*, 92.
3. Eacott, "Memory for the Events of Early Childhood," 46; Waldfogel, "The Frequency and Affective Character," 1.
4. Josselson, "Stability and Change."
5. Adler, *The Science of Living*, 48–57.
6. Clark, *Early Recollections: Theory and Practice*, 52–54.
7. Clark, *Early Recollections: Theory and Practice*, 52–54; Mwita, "Martin Luther King Jr.'s Lifestyle."
8. Carter, *An Hour before Daylight*, 28–29.
9. Brinkley, *The Unfinished Presidency*.
10. Brinkley, *The Unfinished Presidency*.
11. Carter, *Beyond the White House*; Carter, *Our Endangered Values*, 30.

## CHAPTER 2

1. Yeats, *Autobiographies*, 5.
2. Miles, "A Study of Individual Psychology," 535.
3. Miles, "A Study of Individual Psychology," 555.
4. Henri, "Our Earliest Memories," 303–5.
5. Henri and Henri, "Enquête sur les Premiers Souvenirs de L'enfance"; Henri and Henri, "Earliest Recollections."
6. Henri, "Our Earliest Memories," 304.

7. Henri and Henri, "Earliest Recollections," 114.

8. Henri, Victor. "Our Earliest Recollections of Childhood." *Psychological Review* 2 (1895): 215–16.

9. Henri and Henri, "Earliest Recollections," 109.

10. Henri and Henri, "Earliest Recollections," 109.

11. Henri and Henri, "Earliest Recollections," 113.

12. Colegrove, "Individual Memories"; Henri and Henri, "Enquête sur les Premeiers Souvenirs de L'enfance"; Henri and Henri, "Earliest Recollections"; Howe, *The Fate of Early Memories*; Howe, *The Nature of Early Memory*; Kihlstrom and Harackiewicz, "The Earliest Recollection"; Waldfogel, "The Frequency and Affective Character."

13. Crook and Harden, "A Quantitative Investigation," 673–74; Dudycha and Dudycha, "Some Factors and Characteristics," 268; Dudycha and Dudycha, "Childhood Memories," 673–74; Kihlstrom and Harackiewicz, "The Earliest Recollection," 144–45.

14. Dudycha and Dudycha, "Some Factors and Characteristics," 268; Rubin, "The Distribution of Early Childhood Memories," 268; Waldfogel, "The Frequency and Affective Character," 11.

15. Waldfogel, "The Frequency and Affective Character," 11–12.

16. Dudycha and Dudycha, "Adolescents' Memories of Preschool Experiences"; Kihlstrom and Harackiewicz, "The Earliest Recollection"; Waldfogel, "The Frequency and Affective Character"; Westman and Westman, "First Memories."

17. Freud, "The Psychopathology of Everyday Life," 43–52.

18. Colegrove, "Individual Memories," 229.

19. Gordon, "A Study of Early Memories," 130–31.

20. Gordon, "A Study of Early Memories," 132.

21. Epstein, "Social Class Membership"; Pattie and Cornett, "Unpleasantness of Early Memories."

22. Waldfogel, "The Frequency and Affective Character," 18–19.

23. Potwin, "Study of Early Memories," 598; Saunders and Norcross, "Earliest Childhood Memories," 100; Westman and Westman, "First Memories," 329–30.

24. Saunders and Norcross, "Earliest Childhood Memories," 100.

## CHAPTER 3

1. Adler, *What Life Should Mean to You*, 75.

2. Ansbacher, "Adler's Interpretation of Early Recollections," 134–35.

3. Freud, "The Psychopathology of Everyday Life," 43.

4. Adler, *Understanding Human Nature*, 48–49.

5. Ansbacher, "Adler's Interpretation of Early Recollection," 135–36.

6. Sweeney, *Adlerian Counseling and Psychotherapy*, 7–8.

7. Adler, *What Life Should Mean to You*, 73.

8. Adler, *The Science of Living*, 48–49.

9. Adler, *Understanding Human Nature*, 48.

10. Adler, *The Science of Living*, 38–47; Ansbacher, "Life Style."

11. Adler, *What Life Should Mean to You*, 74.

12. Adler, *The Science of Living*, 50–68; Adler, *What Life Should Mean to You*, 86–92.

13. Adler, "Significance of Early Recollections," 284.

14. Adler, *What Life Should Mean to You*, 56–60.

15. Adler, "Significance of Early Recollections," 283.

16. Adler, *Social Interest*; Ansbacher, "Social Interest."

17. Adler, *Social Interest*; Ansbacher, "Social Interest"; Clark, "Empathy and Alfred Adler."

18. Adler, "Significance of Early Recollections," 283.

19. Adler, *Understanding Human Nature*, 60–62; Clark and Simpson, "Imagination."

20. Ansbacher and Ansbacher, *The Individual Psychology of Alfred Adler*, 163–71; Clark and Butler, "Degree of Activity"; Lundin, *Alfred Adler's Basic Concepts*, 49–55.

21. Fried, *Active/Passive*.

22. Ansbacher and Ansbacher, *The Individual Psychology of Alfred Adler*, 164.

23. Adler, "The Fundamental Views of Individual Psychology," 6–8; Ansbacher, "Individual Psychology," 51–52.

24. Adler, "The Fundamental Views of Individual Psychology," 6; Ansbacher, "Individual Psychology," 62.

25. Adler, *What Life Should Mean to You*, 74; Mosak, "Early Recollections," 305.

26. Dreikurs, *Psychodynamics, Psychotherapy, and Counseling*, 10.

27. Adler, *The Science of Living*, 16–17; Sweeney, *Adlerian Counseling and Psychotherapy*, 14–16.

# CHAPTER 4

1. Axline, *Dibs: In Search of Self*, 216.

2. Cosgrove and Ballou, "A Complement to Lifestyle Assessment."

3. Eacott, "Memory for the Events of Early Childhood," 46; Waldfogel, "The Frequency and Affective Character," 1.

4. Adler, *The Science of Living,* 48–57; Adler, "Significance of Early Recollections."

5. Hedvig, "Stability of Early Recollections," 28; Josselson, "Stability and Change."

6. Josselson, "Stability and Change."

7. Clark, "Early Recollections: A Humanistic Assessment"; Clark, "Projective Techniques."

8. Rose, Kaser-Boyd, and Maloney, *Essentials of Rorschach Assessment.*

9. Clark, *Theory and Practice*, 92.

10. Adler, *The Science of Living*, 48.

11. Adler, *What Life Should Mean to You*, 75; Adler, *The Science of Living*; Adler, "Significance of Early Recollections."

12. Adler, "Significance of Early Recollections," 285.

13. Bruhn, "Earliest Childhood Memories"; Clark, *Early Recollections*; Langs, "Earliest Memories and Personality"; Levy, "Early Memories"; Lord, "On the Clinical Use of Children's Early Recollections"; Manaster and Perryman, "Early Recollections and Occupational Choice"; Mayman, "Early Memories and Character Structure"; Powers and Griffith, *Understanding Life-Style.*

14. Adler, *Social Interest*, 212–13; Adler, "Significance of Early Recollections," 284; Clark and Butler, "Degree of Activity"; McCarter, Schiffman, and Tomkins, "Early Recollections as Predictors."

15. Manaster, Berra, and Mays, "Manaster-Perryman Early Recollections Scoring Manual"; Manaster and Perryman, "Occupational Choice."

16. Sweeney and Myers, "Early Recollections: An Adlerian Technique with Older People," 9.

17. Clark, "Early Recollections and Object Meanings."

18. Clark, "An Early Recollection of Albert Einstein."

# CHAPTER 5

1. Huyghe, "Voices, Glances, Flashbacks."

2. Franklin, *A Biography in His Own Words.*

3. Tourtellot, *Benjamin Franklin: The Shaping of a Genius*, 129.

4. Franklin, *A Biography in His Own Words*, 29.

5. Lemay, "The Life of Benjamin Franklin," 29.

6. Van Doren, *Benjamin Franklin*, 110.

7. Franklin, *A Biography in His Own Words*, 153; Van Doren, *Benjamin Franklin*, 109.

8. Keyes, *Ben Franklin: An Affectionate Portrait*, 157; Lemay, "Life of Benjamin Franklin," 39.

9. Isaacson, *Benjamin Franklin: An American Life*, 1–2; Lemay, "Life of Benjamin Franklin," 28; Smith, "Benjamin Franklin, Civic Improver," 91–92.

10. Lemay, "Life of Benjamin Franklin," 36.

11. Lemay, "Life of Benjamin Franklin," 53.

12. Smyth, *The Writings of Benjamin Franklin*, 183–84, 191–92; Van Doren, *Benjamin Franklin*, 8.

13. Clark, *Theory and Practice*, 92.

14. McLaughlin and Ansbacher, "Sane Ben Franklin," 195; Tourtellot, *Shaping of a Genius*, 29.

15. Franklin, *Poor Richard's Almanack*, 493.

16. Tourtellot, *Benjamin Franklin: The Shaping of a Genius*, 129.

17. Isaacson, *Benjamin Franklin: An American Life*, 73.

18. Lemay, "Life of Benjamin Franklin," 27.

19. Clark and Butler, "Degree of Activity."

20. Bruhn, "In Celebration of His 300th Birthday," 38.

21. Ansbacher, "Alfred Adler's Concept"; Adler, *Social Interest*.

22. McLaughlin and Ansbacher, "Sane Ben Franklin."

23. Franklin, *Poor Richard's Almanack*, 466.

24. Aspinwall, Richter, and Hoffman III, "Understanding How Optimism Works."

25. Carver, Scheier, and Segerstrom, "Optimism."

26. Isaacson, *Benjamin Franklin: An American Life*, 490.

27. Ashford, Edmunds, and French, "What Is the Best Way to Change Self-Efficacy?"; Bandura, *Self-Efficacy: The Experience of Control*; Pomeroy and Clark, "Self-Efficacy and Early Recollections."

28. Franklin, *A Biography in His Own Words*, 68; Smith, "Benjamin Franklin, Civic Improver," 108.

29. Keyes, *An Affectionate Portrait*, 63, 69.

30. Roberts, Walton, and Bogg, "Conscientiousness and Health."

31. Franklin, *A Biography in His Own Words*, 83.

32. Lemay, "Life of Benjamin Franklin," 18–19.

33. Franklin, *A Biography in His Own Words*; Keyes, *An Affectionate Portrait*, 62; Van Doren, *Benjamin Franklin*, 69.

34. Franklin, *A Biography in His Own Words*, 73.

35. Clark, "Early Recollections and Sensory Modalities."

36. Isaacson, *Benjamin Franklin: An American Life*, 266; Keyes, *An Affectionate Portrait*, 68; Smyth, *The Writings of Benjamin Franklin*, 210.

37. Clark, "Meaning of Color."

38. Clark, "Experience of Place."

39. Isaacson, *Benjamin Franklin: An American Life*, 487; Tourtellot, *Benjamin Franklin: The Shaping of a Genius*, 133.

40. Tourtellot, *Benjamin Franklin: The Shaping of a Genius*, 130.

41. Clark, "Object Meanings," 124.


## CHAPTER 6


1. Dreikurs, *Psychodynamics, Psychotherapy, and Counseling*, 87.

2. Clark, *Early Recollections*, 104–6.

3. Clark, "Empathy," 349–50.

4. Clark, *Early Recollections*, 92–93; Olson, "Techniques of Interpretation," 71–73.


## CHAPTER 7


1. Christie, *Agatha Christie: An Autobiography*, iii.

2. Adler, *Social Interest*.

3. Adler, "Significance of Early Recollections," 283.

4. Fried, *Active/Passive*, 3–11.

5. Friedman and Martin, *The Longevity Project*, 34–35; Lyubomirsky, *The How of Happiness*, 245.

6. Clark and Butler, "Degree of Activity," 141; Lundin, *Alfred Adler's Basic Concepts*, 49–55.

7. Adler, *Social Interest*.

8. Clark, "Empathy and Alfred Adler," (forthcoming); Clark, A New Model of Empathy in Counseling"; Highland, Kern, and Curlette, "Murderers and Nonviolent Offenders"; Seligman, *Learned Optimism*, 288–90.

9. Adler, "The Fundamental Views of Individual Psychology."

10. Friedman and Martin, *The Longevity Project*, 167.

11. Adler, "Significance of Early Recollections," 283.

12. Scheier, Carver, and Bridges, "Optimism, Pessimism," 191; Marshall, Wortman, Kusulas, Heruing, and Vickers, "Distinguishing Optimism from Pessimism," 1071–72; Tennen and Affleck, "The Costs and Benefits," 382.

13. Aspinwall, Richter, and Hoffman, "Understanding How Optimism Works," 218.

14. Scheier, Carver, and Bridges, "Optimism, Pessimism"; Seligman, *Flourish*, 204–6; Sharot, *The Optimism Bias*, 57.

15. Carver, Scheier, and Segerstrom, "Optimism"; Sharot, *The Optimism Bias*, 58; Zuckerman, "Optimism and Pessimism: Biological Foundations," in *Optimism and Pessimism*, 178–81.

16. Dinter, "The Relationship between Self-Efficacy and Lifestyle Patterns"; Zulkosky, "Self-Efficacy: A Concept Analysis," 94.

17. Ashford, Edmunds, and French, "What Is the Best Way to Change Self-Efficacy"; Bandura, "Health Promotion"; Brady-Amoon and Fuertes, "Self-Efficacy"; Paxton, Motl, Aylward, and Nigg, "Physical Activity and Quality of Life"; Zulkosky, "Self-Efficacy: A Concept Analysis."

18. Bandura, "Self-Efficacy Conception of Anxiety," 100.

19. Bandura, "Human Agency"; Bandura, "Self-Efficacy Conception of Anxiety"; Cervone, "Thinking About Self-Efficacy"; Kelly and Daughtry, "The Role of Recent Stress."

20. Bandura, "Self-Efficacy Conception of Anxiety," 100–101.

21. Jackson, Wood, Bogg, Walton, Harms, and Roberts, "What Do Conscientious People Do?"; McCrae and John, "An Introduction to the Five-Factor Model," 178; McCrae and Costa, *Personality in Adulthood*, 46–47.

22. McCrae and Costa, *Personality in Adulthood*, 46–47, 50–51.

23. Boyce, Wood, and Brown, "The Dark Side of Conscientiousness," 535; McCrae and John, "An Introduction to the Five-Factor Model."

24. Friedman and Martin, *The Longevity Project*, 9, 15; Kern, Friedman, Martin, Reynolds, and Luong, "Conscientiousness, Career Success, and Longevity," 157; O'Connor, Conner, Jones, McMillan, and Ferguson, "Exploring the Benefits of Conscientiousness"; Roberts, Walton, and Bogg, "Conscientiousness and Health,"159–60.

25. Roberts, Walton, and Bogg, "Conscientiousness and Health," 162–163.

26. Roberts, Walton, and Bogg, "Conscientiousness and Health," 157.

27. Lyubomirsky, *The How of Happiness*, 222–25; Seligman, *Flourish*, 125.

28. Clark, *Defense Mechanisms*; Mozdzierz, Peluso, and Lisiecki, *Principles of Counseling and Psychotherapy*, 19–20.

# CHAPTER 8

1. Huxley, *Ends and Means*, 333.

2. Dudycha and Dudycha, "Childhood Memories," 675–76; Henri and Henri, "Earliest Recollections"; Kihlstrom and Harackiewicz, "The Earliest Recollection," 139–40.

3. Clark, "Early Recollections and Sensory Modalities," 363.

4. Potwin, "Study of Early Memories," 598; Saunders and Norcross, "Earliest Childhood Memories," 100; Westman and Wautier, "Early Autobiographical Memories."

5. Clark, "Early Recollections and Sensory Modalities," 363–64.

6. Kabat-Zinn, *Coming to Our Senses*, 221–23; Montagu, *Touching*; Thayer, "Social Touching," 267–72.

7. Saunders and Norcross, "Earliest Childhood Memories," 100; Westman and Orellana, 532; Westman, Westman, and Orellana, "Earliest Memories and Recall by Modality."

8. Clark, "Early Recollections and Sensory Modalities," 357–58.

9. Laird, "What Can You Do with Your Nose?" 126; Schab, "Odors," 648.

10. Gibbons, "The Intimate Sense of Smell," 324.

11. Kihlstrom and Harackiewicz, "The Earliest Recollection," 139; Westman and Westman, "First Memories," 329.

12. Clark, "Early Recollections and Sensory Modalities," 359.

13. Cowart, "Development of Taste Perception in Humans"; Kihlstrom and Harackiewicz, "The Earliest Recollection," 139; Saunders and Norcross, "Earliest Childhood Memories," 100.

14. Ramachandran and Hubbard, "Hearing Colors, Tasting Shapes."

15. Ackerman, *A Natural History of the Senses*, 287–99; Ramachandran and Hubbard, "Hearing Colors, Tasting Shapes," 83.

16. Ramachandran and Hubbard, "Hearing Colors, Tasting Shapes," 78.

17. Williams and Bonvillian, "Early Childhood Memories in Deaf and Hearing College Students."

18. Heller, "Haptic Perception in Blind People," 240.

19. Heller, "Haptic Perception in Blind People," 245–47.

20. Clark, "On the Meaning of Color," 142.

21. Clark, "On the Meaning of Color," 148–50.

22. Clark, "Early Recollections and the Experience of Place," 215.

23. Clark, "Early Recollections and the Experience of Place," 215; Stewart, "Individual Psychology and Environmental Psychology," 73.

24. Hay, "Sense of Place in Developmental Context"; Holmes, Patterson, and Stalling, "Sense of Place."

25. Clark, "Early Recollections and Object Meanings," 124.

26. Clark, "Early Recollections and Object Meanings," 130–31.

27. Cohen and Clark, "Transitional Object Attachment"; Winnicott, "Transitional Objects and Transitional Phenomena."

# CHAPTER 9

1. Wrigley, *Winston Churchill*, xxiv.

2. Clark, *Early Recollections: Theory and Practice in Counseling and Psychotherapy*, 52–54; Mwita, "Martin Luther King Jr.'s Lifestyle."

3. Cunningham, *In Pursuit of Reason*, 2.

4. Meacham, *Thomas Jefferson: The Art of Power*, 137–43; Randall, *Thomas Jefferson: A Life*.

5. Ellis, *American Sphinx*, 271; Risjord, *Jefferson's America*.

6. Randolph, *The Domestic Life of Thomas Jefferson*.

7. Randolph, *The Domestic Life of Thomas Jefferson*, 23.

8. Randolph, *The Domestic Life of Thomas Jefferson*, 23.

9. Ellis, *American Sphinx*, 45.

10. Cunningham, *In Pursuit of Reason*, 5.

11. Kelly-Gangi, *Thomas Jefferson*, 8.

12. Hatch and Waters, *A Rich Spot of Earth*.

13. Cunningham, *In Pursuit of Reason*, 343.

14. Cunningham, *In Pursuit of Reason*, 134.

15. Gordon-Reed, *The Hemingses of Monticello*, 94.

16. Ellis, *American Sphinx*, 280; Gordon-Reed, *The Hemingses of Monticello*, 94; Randall, *Life of Thomas Jefferson*, 11.

17. Gordon-Reed, *The Hemingses of Monticello*.

18. Randall, *Life of Thomas Jefferson*, 474.

19. Ellis, *American Sphinx*, 344.

20. Meacham, *Thomas Jefferson: The Art of Power*, 425–35; Randall, *Thomas Jefferson: A Life*, 579–83.

21. Boyd et al., *The Papers of Thomas Jefferson*, 10.

22. Cunningham, *In Pursuit of Reason*, 323.

23. Cunningham, *In Pursuit of Reason*, 333.

24. Ellis, *American Sphinx*, 45.

25. White and Gribbin, *Einstein: A Life in Science*.

26. Clark, "Early Recollection of Albert Einstein."

27. Einstein, *Ideas and Opinions*.

28. Einstein, *Autobiographical Notes*.

29. Isaacson, *Einstein: His Life and Universe*, 548.

30. Einstein, *Ideas and Opinions*, 11.

31. Isaacson, *Einstein: His Life and Universe*, 367.

32. Isaacson, *Einstein: His Life and Universe*, 358.

33. White and Gribbin, *Einstein: A Life in Science*.

34. Isaacson, *Einstein: His Life and Universe*, 67.

35. Isaacson, *Einstein: His Life and Universe*, 393.

36. Isaacson, *Einstein: His Life and Universe*, 367.

37. Isaacson, *Einstein: His Life and Universe*, 520.

38. Isaacson, *Einstein: His Life and Universe*, 441.

39. Isaacson, *Einstein: His Life and Universe*, 9.

40. Brian, *Einstein: A Life*, 185–86.

41. Einstein, *Ideas and Opinions*, 8.

42. Teresa, *Mother Teresa: Come Be My Light*, 14.

43. Teresa, *Mother Teresa: Come Be My Light*, 40; Royle and Woods, *Mother Theresa: A Life in Pictures*, 21.

44. Teresa, *Mother Teresa: Come Be My Light*, 139.

45. Teresa, Mother. *Mother Teresa: No Greater Love*. Edited by Becky Benenate and Joseph Durepos. Novato, CA: New World Library, 1997, 309.

46. Royle and Woods, *Mother Teresa: A Life in Pictures*, 39.

47. Teresa, *Mother Teresa: Where There Is Love*, 291; Royle and Woods, *Mother Theresa: A Life in Pictures*, 47–48.

48. Teresa, *Mother Teresa: Come Be My Light*, 333.

49. Teresa, *Mother Teresa: Where There Is Love*, 79.

50. Teresa, *Mother Teresa: Where There Is Love*, xii.

51. Spink, *Mother Teresa*, 35; Vazhakala, *Life with Mother Teresa*, 84.

52. Teresa, *Mother Teresa: Come Be My Light*, 34.

53. Teresa, *No Greater Love*, 66.

54. Teresa, *No Greater Love*, 90.

55. Teresa, *No Greater Love*, 28.

56. Teresa, *Mother Teresa: Come Be My Light*, 233.

57. Teresa, *Mother Teresa: Come Be My Light*, 121, 131.

58. Teresa, *Mother Teresa: Come Be My Light*, 21–22, 157–58.

59. Vazhakala, *Life with Mother Teresa*, 122.

60. Teresa, *Mother Teresa: Where There Is Love*, 93.

61. Teresa, *Mother Teresa: Where There Is Love*, 83.

62. Royle and Woods, *Mother Teresa: A Life in Pictures*, 19; Spink, *Mother Teresa*, 8.

63. Teresa, *Mother Teresa: Where There Is Love*, 337–38.

64. Teresa, *Mother Teresa: Come Be My Light*, 170.

65. Teresa, *Mother Teresa: Where There Is Love*, 245.

# CHAPTER 10

1. May, *Man's Search for Himself*, 258.

2. Clark, *Early Recollections: Theory and Practice*, 57–75.

3. Manaster and Corsini, *Individual Psychology*, 179, 189.

4. Ladd and Churchill, *Person-Centered Diagnosis*, 60–61; Segal, "Appraisal of the Self-Schema Construct."

5. Carlson and Dinkmeyer, "Couple Therapy"; Deaner and Pechersky, "Early Recollections: Enhancing Case Conceptionalization"; Eckstein, Welch, and Gam-

ber, "The Process of Early Recollections (PERR) for Couples and Families"; Hawes, "Early Recollections: A Compelling Intervention in Couples Therapy"; Peluso and MacIntosh, "Emotionally Focused Couples Therapy," 259–60.

6. Bruhn, "Children's Earliest Memories"; Clark, "Early Recollections: A Personality Assessment Tool"; Janoe, "Using Early Recollections"; LaFountain and Gardner, *A School with Solutions*, 67–72, 81–85; Myer and James, "Early Recollections"; Statton and Wilborn, "Adlerian Counseling"; Watkins and Schatman, "Using Early Recollections in Child Psychotherapy."

7. Sweeney, "Early Recollections: A Promising Technique"; Sweeney and Myers, "Early Recollections: An Adlerian Technique with Older People."

8. Hafner and Fakouri, "Early Recollections and Vocational Choice"; Manaster and Perryman, "Early Recollections and Occupational Choice"; McKelvie, "Career Counseling with Early Recollections"; Watkins, "Using Early Recollections in Career Counseling"; Watts and Engels, "The Life Task of Vocation."

9. Attarian, "Early Recollections: Predictors of Vocational Choice"; Watkins, "Using Early Recollections in Career Counseling."

10. Crites, *Vocational Psychology*, 408–68.

11. Clark, *Empathy in Counseling and Psychotherapy*, 187–210; Clark, "A New Model of Empathy in Counseling"; Egan, *The Skilled Helper*, 104 –33; Ivey, Ivey, and Zalaquett, *Essentials of Intentional Interviewing*, 131–34; Sommers-Flanagan and Sommers-Flanagan, *Counseling and Psychotherapy Theories*, 161–62; Young, *Learning the Art of Helping*, 19–20, 58–60.

# CHAPTER 11

1. Hampl, *A Romantic Education*, 5.

2. Estrade, *You Are What You Remember*; Leman, *What Your Childhood Memories Say About You*; Leman and Carlson, *Unlocking the Secrets of Your Childhood*; Singer, *Memories That Matter*.

# Bibliography

Ackerman, Diane. *A Natural History of the Senses*. New York: Vintage Books, 1995.

Adler, Alfred. *The Practice and Theory of Individual Psychology*. 1920. Translated by P. Radin. Totowa, NJ: Littlefield, Adams, 1968.

———. *Understanding Human Nature*. Translated by Walter Beran Wolfe and Leland E. Hinsie. New York: Greenberg, 1927.

———. *The Pattern of Life*. 1930. 2nd ed. Edited by Walter Beran Wolfe. Chicago: Alfred Adler Institute of Chicago, 1982.

———. "The Fundamental Views of Individual Psychology." *International Journal of Individual Psychology* 1, no. 1 (1935): 5–8.

———. "Significance of Early Recollections." *International Journal of Individual Psychology* 3, no. 4 (1937): 283–87.

———. *What Life Should Mean to You*. 1931. Edited by Alan Porter. New York: Capricorn Books, 1958.

———. *Social Interest: A Challenge to Mankind*. 1933. Translated by John Linton and Richard Vaughn. New York: Capricorn Books, 1964.

———. *The Science of Living*. 1929. Edited by Heinz L. Ansbacher. Garden City, NY: Anchor Books, 1969.

Ansbacher, Heinz L. "Life Style: A Historical and Systematic Review." *Journal of Individual Psychology* 23, no. 2 (1967): 191–203.

———. "Adler's Interpretation of Early Recollections: Historical Account." *Journal of Individual Psychology* 29, no. 2 (1973): 135–45.

———. "Individual Psychology." In *Contemporary Personality Theories*, edited by Raymond Corsini, 45–82. Itasca, IL: F. E. Peacock, 1977.

———. "The Concept of Social Interest." *Individual Psychology: The Journal of Adlerian Theory, Research and Practice* 71, no. 1 (1991): 28–46.

———. "Alfred Adler's Concepts of Social Interest and Community Feeling and the Relevance of Community Feeling for Old Age." *Individual Psychology: The Journal of Adlerian Theory, Research, and Practice* 48, no. 4 (1992): 402–12.

Ansbacher, Heinz L., and Rowena R. Ansbacher, eds. *The Individual Psychology of Alfred Adler: A Systematic Presentation in Selections from His Writings.* New York: Basic Books, 1956.

Ashford, Stefanie, Jemma Edmunds, and David P. French. "What Is the Best Way to Change Self-Efficacy to Promote Lifestyle and Recreational Physical Activity?: A Systematic Review with Meta-Analysis." *British Journal of Health Psychology* 15, no. 2 (2010): 265–88.

Aspinwall, Lisa G., Linda Richter, and Richard R. Hoffman III. "Understanding How Optimism Works: An Examination of Optimists' Adaptive Moderation of Belief and Behavior." In *Optimism and Pessimism Implications for Theory, Research, and Practice*, edited by Edward C. Chang, 217–38. Washington, DC: American Psychological Association, 2001.

Attarian, Peter J. "Early Recollections: Predictors of Vocational Choice." *Journal of Individual Psychology* 34, no. 1 (1978): 56–62.

Axline, Virginia M. *Dibs: In Search of Self.* New York: Ballantine Books, 1964.

Baldwin, Christina. *One to One: Self-Understanding through Journal Writing.* New York: M. Evans, 1977.

Bandura, Albert. "Human Agency in Social Cognitive Therapy." *American Psychologist* 44, no. 9 (1989): 1175–84.

———. "Self-Efficacy Conception of Anxiety." In *Anxiety and Self-Focused Attention*, edited by Ralf Schwarzer and Robert A. Wicklund, 89–110. New York: Harwood Academic Publishers, 1991.

———. *Self-Efficacy: The Experience of Control.* New York: Freeman, 1997.

———. "Health Promotion by Social Cognitive Means." *Health Education and Behavior* 31, no. 2 (2004): 143–64.

Boyce, Christopher J., Alex M. Wood, and Gordon D. A. Brown. "The Dark Side of Conscientiousness: Conscientious People Experience Greater Drops in Life Satisfaction Following Unemployment." *Journal of Research in Personality* 44, no. 4 (2010): 535–39.

Boyd, Julian P. *The Papers of Thomas Jefferson.* Princeton, NJ: Princeton University Press, 1950.

Brady-Amoon, Peggy, and Jairo N. Fuertes. "Self-Efficacy, Self-Rated Abilities, Adjustment, and Academic Performance." *Journal of Counseling and Development* 89, no. 4 (2011): 431–38.

Brian, Denis. *Einstein: A Life.* New York: John Wiley and Sons, 1996.

Brinkley, Douglas. *The Unfinished Presidency: Jimmy Carter's Journey beyond the White House.* New York: Viking, 1998.

Brown, Jonathan D., and Margaret A. Marshall. "Great Expectations: Optimism and Pessimism in Achievement Settings." In *Optimism and Pessimism: Implications for Theory, Research, and Practice*, edited by Edward C. Chang, 239–55. Washington, DC: American Psychological Association, 2001.

Bruhn, Arnold Rahn. "Children's Earliest Memories: Their Use in Clinical Practice. *Journal of Personality Assessment* 45, no. 3 (1981): 258–62.

———. *Earliest Childhood Memories: Theory and Application to Clinical Practice*, Vol. 1. New York: Praeger, 1990.

———. "In Celebration of His 300th Birthday: Benjamin Franklin's Early Memories Procedure." *E-Journal of Applied Psychology: Clinical and Social Issues* 2, no. 1 (2006): 22–44.

Carlson, Jon, and Donald Dinkmeyer Sr. "Couple Therapy." In *Interventions and Strategies in Counseling and Psychotherapy*, edited by Richard E. Watts and Jon Carlson, 87–100. Philadelphia: Accelerated Development, 1999.

Carter, Jimmy. *An Hour before Daylight: Memories of a Rural Boyhood.* New York: Touchstone, 2001.

———. *Our Endangered Values: America's Moral Crisis.* New York: Simon and Schuster, 2005.

———. *Beyond the White House: Waging Peace, Fighting Disease, Building Hope.* New York: Simon and Schuster, 2007.

Carver, Charles S., Michael F. Scheier, and Suzanne C. Segerstrom. "Optimism." *Clinical Psychology Review* 30, no. 7 (2010): 879–89.

Cervone, Daniel. "Thinking about Self-Efficacy." *Behavior Modification* 24, no. 1 (2000): 30–56.

Christie, Agatha. *Agatha Christie: An Autobiography.* New York: Ballatine Books, 1977.

Clark, Arthur J. "Early Recollections: A Personality Assessment Tool for Elementary School Counselors." *Elementary School Guidance and Counseling* 29, no. 2 (1994): 92–101.

———. "Projective Techniques in the Counseling Process." *Journal of Counseling and Development* 73, no. 3 (1995): 311–16.

———. *Defense Mechanisms in the Counseling Process.* Thousand Oaks, CA: Sage, 1998.

———. "Early Recollections: A Humanistic Assessment in Counseling." *Journal of Humanistic Counseling, Education, and Development* 40, no. 1 (2001): 96–104.

———. *Early Recollections: Theory and Practice in Counseling and Psychotherapy.* New York: Brunner-Routledge, 2002.

———. "On the Meaning of Color in Early Recollections." *The Journal of Individual Psychology* 60, no. 2 (2004): 141–54.

———. "An Early Recollection of Albert Einstein: Perspectives on Its Meaning and His Life." *The Journal of Individual Psychology* 51, no. 2 (2005): 126–36.

——. "Early Recollections and the Experience of Place." *The Journal of Individual Psychology* 63, no. 2 (2007): 214–24.

——. *Empathy in Counseling and Psychotherapy: Perspectives and Practices.* Mahwah, NJ: Lawrence Erlbaum Associates, 2007.

——. "Early Recollections and Sensory Modalities." *The Journal of Individual Psychology* 64, no. 3 (2008): 353–68.

——. "Early Recollections and Object Meanings." *The Journal of Individual Psychology* 65, no. 2 (2009): 123–34.

——. "A New Model of Empathy in Counseling." *Counseling Today* 52, no. 3 (2009): 46–47.

——. "Empathy: An Integral Model in the Counseling Process." *Journal of Counseling and Development* 88, no. 3 (2010): 348–56.

——. "Significance of Early Recollections." In *Alfred Adler Revisited*, edited by Jon Carlson and Michael Maniacci, 303–6. New York: Routledge, 2012.

——. "Empathy and Alfred Adler." *The Journal of Individual Psychology* (forthcoming).

Clark, Arthur J., and Carrie M. Butler. "Degree of Activity: Relationship to Early Recollections and Safeguarding Tendencies." *The Journal of Individual Psychology* 68, no. 2 (2012): 136–47.

Clark, Arthur J., and Tara M. Simpson. "Imagination an Essential Dimension of a Counselor's Empathy." *Journal of Humanistic Counseling* (forthcoming).

Cohen, Keith N., and James A. Clark. "Transitional Object Attachment in Early Childhood and Personality Characteristics in Later Life." *Journal of Personality and Social Psychology* 46, no. 1 (1984): 106–11.

Colegrove, F. W. "Individual Memories." *American Journal of Psychology* 10, no. 2 (1899): 228–55.

Cosgrove, Sara Anne, and Roger A. Ballou. "A Complement to Lifestyle Assessment: Using Montessori Sensorial Experiences to Enhance and Intensify Early Recollections." *The Journal of Individual Psychology* 62, no. 1 (2006): 47–58.

Cowart, Beverly J. "Development of Taste and Perception in Humans: Sensitivity and Preference throughout the Life Span." *Psychological Bulletin* 90, no. 1 (1981): 43–73.

Crites, John O. *Vocational Psychology: The Study of Vocational Behavior and Development.* New York: McGraw-Hill, 1969.

Crook, Mason N., and Luberta Harden. "A Quantitative Investigation of Early Memories." *Journal of Social Psychology* 2, no. 2 (1931): 252–55.

Cunningham, Noble E., Jr. *In Pursuit of Reason: The Life of Thomas Jefferson.* New York: Ballantine Books, 1988.

Deaner, Richard G., and Kara Pechersky. "Early Recollections: Enhancing Case Conceptionalization for Practitioners Working with Couples." *The Family Journal: Counseling and Therapy for Couples and Families* 13, no. 3 (2005): 311–15.

Dinter, Lynda D. "The Relationship between Self-Efficacy and Lifestyle Patterns." *The Journal of Individual Psychology* 56, no. 4 (2000): 462–73.

Dreikurs, Rudolph. *Psychodynamics, Psychotherapy, and Counseling: Collected Papers of Rudolph Dreikurs.* Chicago: Alfred Adler Institute of Chicago, 1967.

Dudycha, George J., and Martha Malek Dudycha. "Adolescents' Memories of Pre-school Experiences." *Journal of Genetic Psychology* 42 (1933): 468–80.

———. "Some Factors and Characteristics of Childhood Memories." *Child Development* 4, no. 3 (1933): 265–78.

———. "Childhood Memories: A Review of the Literature." *Psychological Bulletin* 38, no. 8 (1941): 668–82.

Dukas, Helen, and Banesh Hoffmann. *Albert Einstein: The Human Side.* Princeton, NJ: Princeton University Press, 1979.

Eacott, Madeline J. "Memory for the Events of Early Childhood." *Current Directions in Psychological Science* 8, no. 2 (1999): 46–49.

Eckstein, Daniel, Deborah V. Welch, and Victoria Gamber. "The Process of Early Recollection Reflection (PERR) for Couples and Families." *Family Journal* 9, no. 2 (2001): 203–9.

Egan, Gerald. *The Skilled Helper: A Problem-Management and Opportunity-Development Approach to Helping.* 10th ed. Belmont, CA: Brooks/Cole, Cengage Learning, 2009.

Einstein, Albert. "Autobiographical Notes." In *Albert Einstein: Philosopher-Scientist*, edited by Paul A. Schilpp, 3–95. Evanston, IL: The Library of Living Philosophers, 1949.

———. *Ideas and Opinions.* Translated by Sonja Bargmann. New York: Crown Publishers, 1954.

Ellenberger, Henri F. *The Discovery of the Unconscious.* New York: Basic Books, 1970.

Ellis, Joseph J. *American Sphinx: The Character of Thomas Jefferson.* New York: Vintage Book, 1998.

Engen, Trygg. *Odor Sensation and Memory.* New York: Praeger, 1991.

Epstein, Ralph. "Social Class Membership and Early Childhood Memories." *Child Development* 34, no. 2 (1963): 503–8.

Estrade, Patrick. *You Are What You Remember: A Pathbreaking Guide to Understanding and Interpreting Your Childhood Memories.* Translated by Leah Laffont. Philadelphia: Da Capo Press, 2008.

Fleming, Thomas, ed. *Benjamin Franklin: A Biography in His Own Words.* Vols. 1 and 2. New York: Newsweek, 1972.

Franklin, Benjamin. *Autobiography, Poor Richard, and Later Writings: Letters from London, 1757–1775, Paris, 1776–1785, Philadelphia 1785–1790, Poor Richard's Almanack, 1733–1758, the Autobiography.* New York: The Library of America, 1997.

Fried, Edrita. *Active/Passive: The Crucial Psychological Dimension.* 1970. New York: Brunner/Mazel, 1989.

Friedman, Howard S., and Leslie R. Martin. *The Longevity Project: Surprising Discoveries for Health and Long Life from the Landmark Eight-Decade Study.* New York: Hudson Street Press, 2011.

Freud, Sigmund. "The Psychopathology of Everyday Life." 1901. In *The Standard Edition of the Complete Psychological Works of Sigmund Freud,* edited and translated by J. Strachey, 43–52. London: Hogarth, 1960.

Gibbons, Boyd. "The Intimate Sense of Smell." *National Geographic* 170, no. 3 (1986): 324–61.

Gordon, Kate. "A Study of Early Memories." *Journal of Delinquency* 12 (1928): 129–32.

Gordon-Reed, Annette. *The Hemingses of Monticello: An American Family.* New York: W.W. Norton, 2008.

Hafner, James L., and M. Ebrahim Fakouri. "Early Recollections and Vocational Choice." *Individual Psychology: The Journal of Adlerian Theory, Research, and Practice* 40, no. 1 (1984): 54–60.

Hampl, Patricia. *A Romantic Education.* Boston: Houghton Mifflin, 1981.

Hatch, Peter J., and Alice Waters. *A Rich Spot of Earth: Thomas Jefferson's Revolutionary Garden at Monticello.* New Haven, CT: Yale University Press.

Hawes, Clair. "Early Recollections: A Compelling Intervention in Couples Therapy." *The Journal of Individual Psychology* 63, no. 3 (2007): 306–14.

Hay, R. "Sense of Place in Developmental Context." *Journal of Environmental Psychology* 18, no. 1 (1998): 2–29.

Hedvig, Eleanor B. "Stability of Early Recollections and Thematic Apperception Stories." *Journal of Individual Psychology* 19, no. 1 (1965): 49–54.

Heller, Morton A. "Haptic Perception in Blind People." In *The Psychology of Touch,* edited by Morton A. Heller and William Schiff, 239–61. Hillsdale, NJ: Lawrence Erlbaum Associates, 1991.

Henri, Victor. "Our Earliest Memories." *American Journal of Psychology* 7, no. 2 (1895): 303–5.

———. "Our Earliest Recollections of Childhood." *Psychological Review* 2 (1895): 215–16.

Henri, Victor, and Catherine Henri. "Enquête sur les Premiers Souvenirs de L'enfance," *Année Psychologique* 3 (1896): 184–98.

Henri, Victor, and Catherine Henri. "Earliest Recollections." *Popular Science Monthly* 53 (1898): 108–15.

Highland, Richard A., Roy M. Kern, and William L. Curlette. "Murderers and Nonviolent Offenders: A Test of Alfred Adler's Theory of Crime. *The Journal of Individual Psychology* 66, no. 4 (2010): 433–58.

Holmes, Gary E., James R. Patterson, and Janice E. Stalling. "Sense of Place: Issues in Counseling and Development." *Journal of Humanistic Counseling, Education, and Development* 42, no. 2 (2003): 238–51.

Howe, Mark L. *The Fate of Early Memories: Developmental Science and the Retention of Childhood Experiences.* Washington, DC: American Psychological Association, 2000.

———. *The Nature of Early Memory: An Adaptive Theory of the Genesis and Development of Memory.* Oxford: Oxford University Press, 2011.

Huxley, Aldous. *Ends and Means.* New York: Greenwood Press, 1969.

Huyghe, Patrick. "Voices, Glances, Flashbacks: Our First Memories." *Psychology Today* 19 (September 1985): 48–52.

Isaacson, Walter. *Benjamin Franklin: An American Life.* New York: Simon and Schuster Paperbacks, 2003.

Isaacson, Walter. *Einstein: His Life and Universe.* New York: Simon and Schuster, 2007.

Ivey, Allen E., Mary Bradford Ivey, and Carlos P. Zalaquett. *Essentials of Intentional Interviewing: Counseling in a Multicultural World.* 2nd ed. Belmont, CA: Brooks/Cole, Cengage Learning, 2012.

Jackson, Joshua J., D. Wood, T. Bogg, K. E. Walton, P. D. Harms, and B. W. Roberts. "What Do Conscientiousness People Do? Development and Validation of the Behavioral Indicators of Conscientiousness (BIC)." *Journal of Research in Personality* 44, no. 4 (2010): 501–11.

Janoe, Barbara, ed. "Using Early Recollections with Children." In *Early Recollections: Their Use in Diagnosis and Psychotherapy*, edited by Harry A. Olson, 230–34. Springfield, IL: Charles C Thomas, 1979.

Josselson, Ruthellen. "Stability and Change in Early Memories over 22 Years: Themes, Variations, and Cadenzas." *Bulletin of the Menninger Clinic* 64, no. 4 (2000): 462–81.

Kabat-Zinn, Jon. *Coming to Our Senses: Healing Ourselves and the World through Mindfulness.* New York: Hyperion, 2005.

Kelly, William E., and Don Daughtry. "The Role of Recent Stress in the Relationship between Worry and Self-Efficacy: Path Analysis of a Meditation Model." *Psychology Journal* 8, no. 4 (2011): 143–48.

Kelly-Gangi, Carol, ed. *Thomas Jefferson: His Essential Wisdom.* New York: Fall River Press, 2010.

Kern, Margaret, L., H. S. Friedman, L. R. Martin, C. A. Reynolds, and G. Luong. "Conscientiousness, Career Success, and Longevity: A Lifespan Analysis." *Annals of Behavioral Medicine* 37, no. 2 (2009): 154–63.

Keyes, Nelson Beecher. *Ben Franklin: An Affectionate Portrait.* Garden City, NY: Hanover House, 1956.

Kihlstrom, John F., and Judith M. Harackiewicz. "The Earliest Recollection: A New Survey." *Journal of Personality* 50, no. 2 (1982): 134–48.

Ladd, Peter D., and AnnMarie Churchill. *Person-Centered Diagnosis and Treatment in Mental Health: A Model for Empowering Clients.* Philadelphia: Jessica Kingsley Publishers.

LaFountain, Rebecca M., and Nadine E. Gardner. *A School with Solutions: Implementing a Solution-Focused/Adlerian-Based Comprehensive School Counseling Program.* Alexandria, VA: American School Counselor Association, 1998.

Laird, Donald A. "What Can You Do with Your Nose?" *Scientific Monthly* 41, no. 2 (1935): 126–30.

Langs, Robert J. "Earliest Memories and Personality: A Predictive Study." *Archives of General Psychiatry* 12, no. 4 (1965): 379–90.

Lemar, Kevin. *What Your Childhood Memories Say About You . . . And What You Can Do About It.* Carol Stream, IL: Tyndate House Publishers, 2007.

Leman, Kevin, and Randy Carlson. *Unlocking the Secrets of Your Childhood Memories.* Nashville, TN: Thomas Nelson, 1989.

Lemay, J. A. Leo. "The Life of Benjamin Franklin." In *Benjamin Franklin: In Search for a Better World*, edited by Page Talbot, 17–54. New Haven, CT: Yale University Press, 2005.

Levy, Joshua. "Early Memories: Theoretical Aspects and Applications." *Journal of Projective Techniques and Personality Assessment* 29, no. 3 (1965): 281–91.

Lord, Daniel B. "On the Clinical Use of Children's Early Recollections." *Individual Psychology: Journal of Adlerian Theory, Research, and Practice* 38, no. 3 (1982): 198–206.

Lundin, Robert W. *Alfred Adler's Basic Concepts and Implications.* Muncie, IN: Accelerated Development, 1989.

Lundy, Allan, and Timothy Potts. "Recollection of a Transitional Object and Needs for Intimacy and Affiliation in Adolescents." *Psychological Reports* 60, no. 3 (1987): 767–73.

Lyubomirsky, Sonja. *The How of Happiness: A New Approach to Getting the Life You Want.* New York: Penguin Books, 2007.

Maddux, James E., Lawrence Brawley, and Angela Boykin. "Self-Efficacy and Healthy Behavior: Prevention, Promotion, and Detection." In *Self-Efficacy, Adaptation, and Adjustment: Theory, Research, and Application*, edited by James E. Maddux, 173–202. New York: Plenum Press, 1995.

Manaster, Guy J., and Raymond J. Corsini. *Individual Psychology: Theory and Practice.* Itasca, IL: F. E. Peacock, 1982.

Manaster, Guy J., and Thomas B. Perryman. "Early Recollections and Occupational Choice." *Journal of Individual Psychology* 30, no. 2 (1974): 232–37.

Manaster, Guy J., Steven Berra, and Mark Mays. "Manaster-Perryman Early Recollections Scoring Manual: Findings and Summary." *The Journal of Individual Psychology* 57, no. 4 (2001): 413–19.

Marshall, Grant N., C. B. Wortman, J. W. Kusulas, L. K. Hervig, and R. R. Vickers Jr. "Distinguishing Optimism from Pessimism: Relations to Fundamental Dimensions of Mood and Personality." *Journal of Personality and Social Psychology* 62, no. 6 (1992): 1067–74.

May, Rollo. *Man's Search for Himself.* New York: W.W. Norton, 1953.

Mayman, Martin. "Early Memories and Character Structure." *Journal of Projective Techniques* 32, no. 4 (1968): 303–16.

McCarter, Robert E., Harold M. Schiffman, and Silvan S. Tomkins. "Early Recollections as Predictors of Tomkins-Horn Picture Arrangement Test Performance. *Journal of Individual Psychology* 17, No. 2 (1961): 177–80.

McCrae, Robert R., and Oliver P. John. "An Introduction to the Five-Factor Model and Its Applications." *Journal of Personality* 60, no. 2 (1992): 175–215.

McCrae, Robert R., and Paul T. Costa, eds. *Personality in Adulthood: A Five-Factor Theory of Personality.* 2nd ed. New York: Guilford Press, 2003.

McKelvie, William H. "Career Counseling with Early Recollections." In *Early Recollections: Their Use in Diagnosis and Psychotherapy*, edited by Harry A. Olson, 243–55. Springfield, IL: Charles C Thomas, 1979.

McLaughlin, John J., and Rowena R. Ansbacher. "Sane Ben Franklin: An Adlerian View of His Autobiography." *Journal of Individual Psychology* 27, no. 2 (1971): 189–207.

Meacham, Jon. *Thomas Jefferson: The Art of Power.* New York: Random House, 2012.

Miles, Caroline. "A Study of Individual Psychology." *American Journal of Psychology* 6 (1895): 534–58.

Montagu, Ashley. *Touching: The Human Significance of the Skin.* New York: Columbia University Press, 1971.

Mosak, Harold. "Early Recollections as a Projective Technique." *Journal of Projective Techniques* 22, no. 3 (1958): 307–11.

Mosak, Harold H., and Roger Di Pietro. *Early Recollections: Interpretation Method and Application.* New York: Routledge, 2006.

Mosak, Harold H., and Maniacci, Michael P. *Tactics in Counseling and Psychotherapy.* Itasca, IL: F. E. Peacock, 1998.

Mozdzierz, Gerald J., Paul R. Peluso, and Joseph Lisiecki. *Principles of Counseling and Psychotherapy: Learning the Essential Domains and Non-linear Thinking of Master Practitioners.* New York: Routledge, 2009.

Mwita, Mahiri. "Martin Luther King Jr.'s Lifestyle and Social Interest in His Autobiographical Early Memories." *The Journal of Individual Psychology* 60, no. 2 (2004): 191–203.

Myer, Rick, and Richard K. James. "Using Early Recollections as an Assessment Technique with Children." *Elementary School Guidance and Counseling* 25, no. 3 (1991): 228–32.

Nichols, Frederick Doveton, and Ralph E. Griswold. *Thomas Jefferson: Landscape Architect*. Charlottesville: University Press of Virginia, 1978.

Oberst, Ursula E., and Alan E. Stewart. *Adlerian Psychotherapy: An Advanced Approach to Individual Psychology*. New York: Brunner-Routledge, 2003.

O'Connor, Daryl B., M. Conner, F. Jones, B. McMillian, and E. Ferguson. "Exploring the Benefits of Conscientiousness: An Investigation of the Role of Daily Stressors and Health Behaviors." *Annals of Behavioral Medicine* 37, no. 2 (2009): 184–96.

Olson, Harry A. "Techniques of Interpretation." In *Early Recollections: Their Use in Diagnosis and Psychotherapy*, edited by Harry A. Olson, 69–82. Springfield, IL: Charles C Thomas, 1979.

Olson, Harry A., ed. *Early Recollections: Their Use in Diagnosis and Psychotherapy*. Springfield, IL: Charles C Thomas, 1979.

Pattie, Frank A., and Stephen Cornett. "Unpleasantness of Early Memories and Maladjustment of Children." *Journal of Personality* 20, no. 3 (1952): 315–21.

Paxton, Raheem J., Robert W. Motl, Alison Aylward, and Claudio R. Nigg. "Physical Activity and Quality of Life: The Complementary Influence of Self-Efficacy for Physical Activity and Mental Health Difficulties." *International Journal of Behavioral Medicine* 17, no. 4 (2010): 255–63.

Peluso, Paul R., and Heather MacIntosh. "Emotionally Focused Couples Therapy and Individual Psychology: A Dialogue across Theories." *The Journal of Individual Psychology* 63, no. 3 (2007): 247–69.

Pomeroy, Heather, and Arthur J. Clark. "Self-Efficacy and Early Recollections in the Context of Adlerian and Wellness Theory." *The Journal of Individual Psychology* (forthcoming).

Potwin, Elizabeth Bartlett. "Study of Early Memories." *Psychological Review* 8, no. 6 (1901): 596–601.

Powers, Robert L., and Jane Griffith. *Understanding Life-Style: The Psycho-Clarity Process*. Chicago: The Americas Institute of Adlerian Studies, 1987.

Ramachandran, Vilayanur S., and Edward M. Hubbard. "Hearing Colors, Tasting Shapes." *Scientific American* 16, no. 3 (2006): 76–83.

Randall, Henry S. *The Life of Thomas Jefferson*. 3 Vols. New York: Derby and Jackson, 1858.

Randall, Willard Sterne. *Thomas Jefferson: A Life*. New York: Henry Holt and Company, 1993.

Randolph, Sarah N. 1871. *The Domestic Life of Thomas Jefferson*. Charlottesville: University of Virginia Press, 1978.

Risjord, Norman K. *Jefferson's America, 1760–1815*. 3rd ed. Lanham, MD: Rowman and Littlefield, 2010.

Roberts, Brent W., Kate E. Walton, and Tim Bogg. "Conscientiousness and Health across the Life Course." *Review of General Psychology* 9, no. 2 (2005): 156–68.

Rose, Tara, Nancy Kaser-Boyd, and Michael P. Maloney. *Essentials of Rorschach Assessment*. New York: John Wiley and Sons, 2001.

Royle, Roger, and Gary Woods. *Mother Theresa: A Life in Pictures*. New York: HarperCollins, 1992.

Rubin, David C. "The Distribution of Early Childhood Memories." *Memory* 8, no. 4 (2000): 265–69.

Saunders, Laura M., and John C. Norcross. "Earliest Childhood Memories: Relationship to Ordinal Position, Family Functioning, and Psychiatric Symptomatology." *Individual Psychology: The Journal of Adlerian Theory, Research, and Practice* 44, no. 1 (1988): 95–105.

Schab, Frank R. "Odors and the Remembrance of Things Past." *Journal of Experimental Psychology: Learning, Memory, and Cognition* 16, no. 4 (1990): 648–55.

Scheier, Michael, Charles S. Carver, and Michael W. Bridges. "Optimism, Pessimism, and Psychological Well-Being." In *Optimism and Pessimism: Implications for Theory, Research, and Practice*, edited by Edward C. Chang, 189–216. Washington, DC: American Psychological Association, 2001.

Segal, Zindel V. "Appraisal of the Self-Schema Construct in Cognitive Models of Depression." *Psychological Bulletin* 103, no. 2 (1988): 147–62.

Seligman, Martin E. P. *Learned Optimism: How to Change Your Mind and Your Life*. New York: Vintage Books, 2006.

Seligman, Martin E. P. *Flourish: A Visionary New Understanding of Happiness and Well-Being*. New York: Free Press, 2011.

Sharot, Tali. *The Optimism Bias: A Tour of the Irrationality Positive Brain*. New York: Pantheon Books, 2011.

Singer, Jefferson A. *Memories That Matter: How to Use Self-Defining Memories to Understand and Change Your Life*. Oakland, CA: New Harbinger Publications, 2005.

Smith, Billy G. "Benjamin Franklin, Civic Improver." In *Benjamin Franklin: In Search of a Better World*, edited by Page Talbot, 91–124. New Haven, CT: Yale University Press, 2005.

Smyth, Albert Henry. *The Writings of Benjamin Franklin*. Vol. 1. New York: Macmillan Company, 1905.

Sommers-Flanagan, John, and Rita Sommers-Flanagan, *Counseling and Psychotherapy Theories in Context and Practice: Skills, Strategies, and Techniques*. 2nd ed. New York: John Wiley and Sons, 2012.

Spink, Kathryn. *Mother Teresa: A Complete Authorized Biography*. New York: HarperOne, 1997.

Statton, Jane Ellis, and Bobbie Wilborn. "Adlerian Counseling and the Early Recollections of Children." *The Journal of Individual Psychology* 47, no. 3 (1991): 338–47.

Stewart, Alan E. "Individual Psychology and Environmental Psychology." *The Journal of Individual Psychology* 63, no. 1 (2007): 67–85.

Sweeney, Thomas J. "Early Recollections: A Promising Technique for Use with Older Persons." *Journal of Mental Health Counseling* 12, no. 3 (1990): 260–69.

———. *Adlerian Counseling and Psychotherapy: A Practitioner's Approach*. 5th ed. New York: Routledge, 2009.

Sweeney, Thomas J., and Jane E. Myers. "Early Recollections: An Adlerian Technique with Older People." *Clinical Gerontologist* 4, no. 4 (1986): 3–12.

Tennen, Howard, and Glenn Affleck. "The Costs and Benefits of Optimistic Explanation and Dispositional Optimism." *Journal of Personality* 55, no. 2 (1987): 377–93.

Teresa, Mother. *In the Heart of the World: Thoughts, Stories, and Prayers*. Edited by Becky Benenate. Novato, CA: New World Library, 1997.

———. *Mother Teresa: No Greater Love*. Edited by Becky Benenate and Joseph Durepos. Novato, CA: New World Library, 1997.

———. *Mother Teresa: Come Be My Light: The Private Writings of the "Saint of Calcutta."* Edited by Brian Kolodiejchuk. New York: Doubleday, 2007.

———. *Mother Teresa: Where There Is Love, There Is God*. Edited by Brian Kolodiejchuk. New York: Doubleday, 2010.

Thayer, Stephen. "Social Touching." In *Tactual Perception: A Sourcebook*, edited by William Schiff and Emerson Foulke, 263–304. New York: Cambridge University Press, 1982.

Tourtellot, Arthur Bernon. *Benjamin Franklin: The Shaping of a Genius, The Boston Years*. New York: Doubleday, 1977.

Vancouver, Jeffery B., Charles M. Thompson, E. Casey Tischner, and Dan J. Putka. "Two Studies Examining the Negative Effect of Self-Efficacy on Performance." *Journal of Applied Psychology* 87, no. 3 (2002): 506–16.

Van Doren, Carl. *Benjamin Franklin*. New York: Penguin Books, 1938.

Vazhakala, Sebastian Fr. *Life with Mother Teresa: My Thirty-Year Friendship with the Mother of the Poor*. Cincinnati, OH: St. Anthony Messenger Press, 2004.

Waldfogel, Samuel. "The Frequency and Affective Character of Childhood Memories." *Psychological Monographs: General and Applied* 62 (4, Whole No. 291) 1948.

Watkins, C. Edward, Jr. "Using Early Recollections in Career Counseling." *Vocational Guidance Quarterly* 32, no. 4 (1984): 271–76.

Watkins, C. Edward, Jr., and Michael E. Schatman. "Using Early Recollections in Child Psychotherapy." *Journal of Child and Adolescent Psychotherapy* 3, no. 3 (1986): 207–13.

Watts, Richard E., and Dennis W. Engels. "The Life Task of Vocation: A Review of Adlerian Research Literature." *Texas Counseling Association Journal* 23, no. 1 (1995): 9–20.

Westman, Alida S., and Gary Wautier. "Early Autobiographical Memories Are Mostly Nonverbal and Their Development Is More Likely Continuous Than Discrete." *Psychological Reports* 74, no. 2 (1994): 655–56.

Westman, Alida S., and Ronald S. Westman. "First Memories Are Nonverbal and Emotional, Not Necessarily Talked About or Part of a Recurring Pattern." *Psychological Reports* 73, no. 1 (1993): 328–30.

Westman, Alida S., Ronald S. Westman, and Cosette Orellana. "Earliest Memories and Recall by Modality Usually Involve Recollections of Different Memories: Memories Are Not Amodal." *Perceptual and Motor Skills* 82, no. 3 (1996): 1131–34.

White, Michael, and John Gribbin. *Einstein: A Life in Science.* New York: Dutton, 1994.

Williams, Robert Lee, and John D. Bonvillian. "Early Childhood Memories in Deaf and Hearing College Students." *Merrill-Palmer Quarterly* 35, no. 4 (1989): 483–97.

Winnicott, D. W. "Transitional Objects and Transitional Phenomena: A Study of the First Not-Me Possession." *The International Journal of Psycho-Analysis* 34, no. 2 (1953): 89–97.

Wrigley, Chris. *Winston Churchill: A Biographical Companion.* Santa Barbara, CA: ABC-CLIO, 2002.

Yeats, William Butler. *Autobiographies: Reveries over Childhood and Youth and the Trembling of the Veil.* 1916. New York: Macmillan, 1927.

Young, Mark E. *Learning the Art of Helping: Building Blocks and Techniques.* 5th ed. Upper Saddle River, NJ: Pearson Education, 2013.

Zuckerman, Marvin. "Optimism and Pessimism: Biological Foundations." In *Optimism and Pessimism: Implications for Theory, Research, and Practice*, edited by Edward C. Chang, 69–88. Washington, DC: American Psychological Association, 2001.

Zulkosky, Kristen. "Self-Efficacy: A Concept Analysis." *Nursing Forum* 44, no. 2 (2009): 93–102.

# Index

# About the Author

**Arthur J. Clark** is a professor and coordinator of the Counseling and Human Development Program at St. Lawrence University in Canton, New York. He received his doctorate in counseling from Oklahoma State University in 1974 and has held positions as a school counselor and school psychologist. His professional experience also includes counseling in a substance abuse treatment facility and maintaining a private practice as a licensed psychologist. Dr. Clark is a contributing editor for *The Journal of Individual Psychology*. His numerous publications include *Defense Mechanisms in the Counseling Process* (1998)*, Early Recollections: Theory and Practice in Counseling and Psychotherapy* (2002), and *Empathy in Counseling and Psychotherapy: Perspectives and Practices* (2007). Art lives with his wife, Marybeth, and they have three daughters, Heather, Tara, and Kayla.